SERVANT

THE PERSON GOD USES

RAUL RIES

SOMEBODY
LOVES
YOU

Diamond Bar, California 91765-2449

SERVANT: The Person God Uses

Library of Congress Control Number: 2015937873

Cover Design:
Rex Agagas

Somebody Loves You Publishing
22324 Golden Springs Drive
Diamond Bar, CA 91765-2449
slymg@calvarygs.org
www.calvarygs.org

ISBN: 978-1-934820-23-0

Printed in the United States of America

SERVANT

THE PERSON GOD USES

Table of Contents

INTRODUCTION

What kind of person does God use?

Many of the men and women God used throughout the Bible called themselves servants—bondservants—*doulos* in the Greek. Paul the Apostle opened the Book of Romans like this: *Paul, a bondservant of Jesus Christ, called to be an apostle, separated to the gospel of God* (Romans 1:1). What does it mean to be a *bondservant?* The word *doulos* means, "a slave, bondman, man of servile condition; devoted to another to the disregard of one's own interests." Paul was a slave to Jesus Christ. His life was not his own; he belonged to Jesus, and he willingly made himself a slave to Christ.

Paul is only one example of the person God uses. If we only look at his life, it is easy to assume God only uses men who are great theologians, as Paul was a Pharisee of all Pharisees (Acts 23:6).

However, God also used Peter, who was a fisherman. He was not a student of the Law. As a matter of fact, God used Moses, who was afraid to speak to the people. King David committed adultery with Bathsheba. Mary was just a young teenaged girl when God chose her to bear the Messiah.

Then there were the other disciples…what a motley crew of guys they were. Thomas was a doubter; James and John were known as the Sons of Thunder, need I say more; and Matthew was a tax collector, not the most upstanding citizen in the area.

Throughout the Bible, we often see God chose all kinds of people—men and women—of all ages and backgrounds to serve Him and do His work. None of God's servants were perfect men or women. They were flawed human beings, who were obedient to the call of God—men and women who submitted their wills to the will of God.

In each person God used, there were certain traits, characteristics and beliefs they held onto. They are the same things the Lord looks for in a person He wants to use for the Kingdom of God. As I look at the many things God is looking for in our lives, they come down to three main things: a spiritual foundation, a personal relationship with God and godly character. Simply, He is looking for someone who is living their life with Christ as their standard. They are attempting to be Christ-like—a Christian.

Some people do not believe they have enough talent, skills or gifts to be used by God, but God is interested in who you are more than what you can do. Trust me, if you have the right spiritual foundation, a personal relationship with God and godly character, God wants to use you to do a mighty work for His kingdom.

The question is: are you ready to be used by God…? When God calls you, will you say, like Samuel: *"Speak, for Your servant hears"* (1 Samuel 3:10)?

Chapter 1

The Person God Uses
Understands Salvation

And as it is appointed for men to die once, but after this the
judgment, so Christ was offered once to bear the sins of many.
To those who eagerly wait for Him He will appear a second
time, apart from sin, for salvation.
Hebrews 9:27-28

Jesus Christ came into this world for one reason. Even though
He helped people, healed people and performed miracles—Jesus
really came into the world to save sinners. Through His death,
He gives new life to every person who comes to Him, by faith,
and submits their life to Him. Once we receive His free gift of
salvation, He opens the door to many more blessings. Along with
salvation comes the opportunity to be used by God, as we continue
to grow in our love and knowledge of Him.

Charles Spurgeon once told a story about a well-known preacher.
He said: "The late, venerable and godly Dr. Archibald Alexander
of Princeton had been a preacher of Christ for 60 years and a

Professor of Divinity for 40 years. On his deathbed, he was heard to say to a friend, 'All my theology is reduced to this narrow compass—Jesus Christ came into the world to save sinners.'"

Dr. Alexander based his conclusion on the words of the Apostle Paul to Timothy:

> *And the grace of our Lord was exceedingly abundant, with faith and love which are in Christ Jesus. This is a faithful saying and worthy of all acceptance, that Christ Jesus came into the world to save sinners, of whom I am chief. However, for this reason I obtained mercy, that in me first Jesus Christ might show all longsuffering, as a pattern to those who are going to believe on Him for everlasting life* (1 Timothy 1:14-16).

Paul was a man greatly used by the Lord to spread the Gospel, and he called himself the chief of sinners. Paul was still used by God, because he realized it was not in his power—it was all the Lord. God chooses who He will use, and then He empowers them.

Salvation—A Blessing from God

When people think of blessings from God, they usually think of material possessions, such as: a house, a car, a job, money, etc., but God's biggest blessing to mankind is not a material possession but a spiritual condition. The greatest gift you can ever receive from God is salvation. Think about it—what better blessing is there then to know you have a relationship with God; your sins are forgiven; and you have eternal life with Christ.

God Has Chosen You

God has chosen you to be saved. The Creator of the Universe has chosen you to be His child and to spend eternity with Him. When you played team sports in school, how often were you chosen first? What a horrible feeling it is to be picked last. The Apostle Paul tells us God chose us before He even formed the foundations of the world: *just as He chose us in Him before the foundation of the world, that we should be holy and without blame before Him in love,* (Ephesians 1:4).

God Has Appointed You to Salvation

God's divine purpose for your life is to appoint you to salvation. That should make you feel loved and special. First Thessalonians 5:9 says: *For God did not appoint us to wrath, but to obtain salvation through our Lord Jesus Christ.* If we firmly understood this, we would not have a problem with self-worth or insecurity.

God Keeps You Saved

God keeps us unto salvation. I do not keep myself; He keeps me. I feel so much more secure knowing my salvation is kept by God—I cannot lose it, as long as I am abiding in Him. When you receive God's gift, the Lord saves you from the sins you have committed, will commit and are going to commit. First Peter 1:5 says: *who are kept by the power of God through faith for salvation ready to be revealed in the last time.*

God Rejoices in Your Salvation

There was a party in heaven when you made your commitment to Jesus Christ. First Peter 4:13 says: *but rejoice to the extent that you partake of Christ's sufferings, that when His glory is revealed, you may also be glad with exceeding joy.*

God Wants You to Work Out Your Salvation

Do not take your salvation lightly. Paul told the Philippian church:

> *Therefore, my beloved, as you have always obeyed, not as in my presence only, but now much more in my absence, work out your own salvation with fear and trembling* (Philippians 2:12).

Working out your salvation means you are abiding in Christ. Make sure you are obedient to the Word of God and you are in the Word each day. Do not neglect prayer—in order to abide in Christ, you need to talk to Him on a daily basis.

The Steps Toward Salvation

Salvation is a free gift, available to everyone, but like any gift, it has to be accepted. In order to accept God's free gift of salvation, there are certain steps you must take.

In Matthew 10:32, Jesus tells us the first step to salvation is to confess Him as Lord. *Therefore whoever confesses Me before men, him I will also confess before My Father who is in heaven.*" Then, in Acts 2:21, Peter told the crowd: *'And it shall come to pass that whoever calls on the name of the Lord shall be saved.'* It seems simple and straightforward. If we want God's gift of salvation, we have to acknowledge Christ, who provided our salvation through His death and resurrection.

Once we confess Jesus Christ as Lord, we have to repent of our sins. Jesus said:

> *And Jesus answered and said to them, "Do you suppose that these Galileans were worse sinners than all other Galileans, because they suffered such things? "I tell you, no; but unless you repent you will all likewise perish"* (Luke 13:2-3).

Jesus is telling us, without repentance, we will perish. We cannot continue to live lives of sin and have communion with the Lord. When you come to the place where you recognize you have sinned against God and you repent, God will begin to do a work in your life.

When we come to Jesus, confess Him as Lord and Savior and repent of our sins, we must have faith. We must believe He truly is our Savior and without Him we cannot be saved. It is impossible to please God without faith. John 3:14-18 says:

> *And as Moses lifted up the serpent in the wilderness, even so must the Son of Man be lifted up, that whoever believes in Him should not perish but have eternal life. For God so loved*

the world that He gave His only begotten Son, that whoever believes in Him should not perish but have everlasting life. For God did not send His Son into the world to condemn the world, but that the world through Him might be saved. "He who believes in Him is not condemned; but he who does not believe is condemned already, because he has not believed in the name of the only begotten Son of God."

We must also believe He forgives us of our sins. Many people have a hard time believing God could forgive them for the terrible things they have done. It takes faith to truly believe and understand the forgiveness of God. It goes beyond our logical minds and emotional hearts. That is faith!

The last requirement of salvation is regeneration. When you are born again in the spirit—you are made into a new person. In John 3:3, Jesus told Nicodemus: *"Most assuredly, I say to you, unless one is born again, he cannot see the kingdom of God."*

You still have your fleshly body, your old way of thinking and living residing in you, but you also have God's spirit, heart and mind residing in you. That is why there is a battle between your fleshly nature and your spiritual nature. However, as you abide in Christ, God fills you with the power of the Holy Spirit and enables you to live a life pleasing to Him. In Acts 1:8, Jesus told the Apostles how they would be empowered by the Holy Spirit to serve Him:

"You shall receive power when the Holy Spirit has come upon you. [And then this is what will happen] *You shall*

become witnesses to me in Jerusalem, in all of Judea, in all of Samaria, and into the ends of the whole earth."

It is only through the regeneration of the Spirit we are able to truly serve the Lord in the way He has called us to serve Him.

The Narrow Way to Salvation

God sent His Son, Jesus, to this earth to save sinners. We are all sinners but He came and died on the Cross, so we would be set free from eternal death, and it is a gift from God. It is not something we can earn. It is something we have to accept from the Lord. Even though He came to save all sinners, Jesus told His disciples this, in Luke 13:22-24:

And He went through the cities and villages, teaching, and journeying toward Jerusalem. Then one said to Him, "Lord, are there few who are saved?" And He said to them, "Strive to enter through the narrow gate, for many, I say to you, will seek to enter and will not be able."

This statement seems to contradict what we have been reading about salvation. If Jesus came into the world to save all sinners, why was He telling them few would be saved? When you look at the massive crowds of people who live in our world today, it is mind boggling to think many of them will not enter heaven.

Unfortunately, the masses are not interested in salvation. Since the beginning of time, the unrighteous have always outnumbered the righteous. During the days of Noah, it is estimated there were five billion people on the earth and the majority were living in chaos and sin. Using Noah to speak for Him, God gave the people 120 years to come to repentance but instead of heeding Noah's warnings, they mocked and made fun of the ark he and his family were building. When the judgment of God finally came, only eight people were saved, out of five billion. An incredible amount of people perished. Only Noah and his family were saved—not because the other five billion people did not have a chance to repent and be saved, but because Noah and his family were the only ones who chose to listen to God and accept His gift of salvation.

In Genesis 19, there is another judgment of God; this time upon the cities of Sodom and Gomorrah. Only three people were saved out of all the inhabitants of the city. '   God told Abraham if He had found 10 repentant people in the city, He would have saved both cities. Instead, the people rebelled against God, so everything and everyone in the cities of Sodom and Gomorrah went up in smoke. Once again, the masses were lost and only the few who obeyed God were saved.

We are living in times like the days of Noah or Sodom and Gomorrah. It is not a popular thing to be a Christian. In fact, Christians are often mocked and persecuted around the world and even in the United States, where we have the First Amendment to protect us.

There are few today, as in biblical times, who are seeking salvation from their sins, but it is not God's will for so many to perish. Paul the Apostle said to Timothy:

> *For this is good and acceptable in the sight of God our Savior, who desires all men to be saved and to come to the knowledge of the truth* (1 Timothy 2:3-4).

Notice, God is willing but man is not always willing. God gives mankind free will—and many, many people choose to follow sin rather than God. They want to get to heaven on their own terms—not God's.

The only way any one of us can be saved and go to heaven is by putting our faith and trust in Jesus Christ. That is it. All roads do not lead to heaven. In John 14:6: *Jesus said to him, "I am the way, the truth, and the life. No one comes to the Father except through Me."*

Paul the Apostle, in Acts 4:12, said: *"Nor is there salvation in any other, for there is no other name under heaven given among men by which we must be saved."* You cannot be saved by Mary, Buddha, Krishna, Muhammad, or any other saint or religious leader. The Apostle Paul said: *"For there is one God and one Mediator between God and men, the Man Christ Jesus"* (1 Timothy 2:5).

Jesus Christ is the bridge builder to God, not any other person, religion, or church. Only Jesus Christ can save you from your sins, and only Christ can call you and anoint you to serve in God's kingdom. Without real salvation, God cannot use your life to serve Him. It is impossible.

The Prodigal World

When I think of the many people who are going to hell, because they will not accept God's free gift of salvation, it reminds me of the parable of the prodigal son. In Luke 15, Jesus taught about the young man who took his inheritance from his father and left home. He went out into the world to party and ended up with nothing, spending his entire inheritance.

Instead of going home, he got a job, but he still suffered:

> *Then he went and joined himself to a citizen of that country, and he sent him into his fields to feed swine. And he would gladly have filled his stomach with the pods that the swine ate, and no one gave him anything* (Luke 15:15-16).

Finally, he humbled himself and decided to return home, not as a privileged son but as a servant:

> *I will arise and go to my father, and will say to him, "Father, I have sinned against heaven and before you, and I am no longer worthy to be called your son. Make me like one of your hired servants"* (Luke 15:18-19).

When his father saw him, he was so happy to have his son return, he had a celebration.

> *"But the father said to his servants, 'Bring out the best robe and put it on him, and put a ring on his hand and sandals on his feet. And bring the fatted calf here and kill it, and let us eat and be merry; for this my son was dead and is alive again; he was lost and is found.' And they began to be merry"* (Luke 15:22-23).

God is just like that father. He wants to give you all He has and so often, just like the prodigal son, we live as servants, starving, instead of coming to Christ and accepting His free gift of salvation. In this parable, Christ is telling us, "Give your life to Me and enjoy the blessings of salvation." As you do, you will find the Lord will use your life in tremendous ways!

Chapter 2

The Person God Uses
Has a Repentant Heart

The Lord is not slack concerning His promise, as
some count slackness, but is longsuffering toward us,
not willing that any should perish but that all should
come to repentance.
2 Peter 3:9

When we read our Bibles, we have a great example of a repentant heart in the Apostle Peter. We also have an example of an unrepentant heart in Judas Iscariot. These two men walked with Jesus, throughout His ministry, but only one of them learned what a truly repentant heart was. Both of these men betrayed the Lord, in their own way, but only one of them lived a truly repentant life. The man with the repentant life was a man who was used tremendously by the Lord. Because he repented and his heart was right before the Lord, God used him to further the work of the ministry, and many came to know the Lord.

Before we look at the lives of Peter and Judas, I think it is important to examine the word *repentance* and how the Bible defines it. In the New Testament the word *repentance* in the Greek means "to turn; or to change; or to have a drastic change of mind." In other words, you make a complete U-turn in the direction your life is going. Repentance denotes "a change of place or a change in the condition of the heart". It involves regret or sorrow, accompanied by a true change of heart towards God. When you repent, you have a change of mind about sin. What used to be something you liked or agreed with now becomes something you hate. True repentance brings about a hatred for sin.

Now we know what true repentance is and we have the opportunity to see it in action when we look at the lives of Judas and Peter. In Matthew 26, we see the beginning of two betrayals of Jesus, Judas in Matthew 26:14-16 and Peter in Matthew 26:31-35. Clearly, they will both betray the Lord, but their lives took different turns as one sought repentance and the other did not.

The Life of Judas—Unrepentant

From the Scriptures, we know Judas was one of the twelve apostles, called by God: *Then one of the twelve, called Judas Iscariot, went to the chief priests* (Matthew 26:14). He was the accountant for the group. He kept the money and many say he stole from the money box. He was the one who questioned Mary for using the costly oil to anoint Jesus, because he thought the oil should be sold and the money put into the money box:

But when His disciples saw it, they were indignant, saying, "Why this waste? For this fragrant oil might have been sold for much and given to the poor" (Matthew 26:8-9).

Right after this encounter with Mary and the anointing of Jesus, Judas went to the chief priests and agreed to betray the Lord:

Then one of the twelve, called Judas Iscariot, went to the chief priests and said, "What are you willing to give me if I deliver Him to you?" And they counted out to him thirty pieces of silver. So from that time he sought opportunity to betray Him (Matthew 26:14-16).

I think it is important to look at the mindset of Judas. He was conspiring to betray the Lord. He did not betray the Lord because he was in danger or as a "heat of the moment" action. He planned and schemed to betray the Lord. This is important, because God looks at the motive of our hearts. Judas clearly was motivated by greed. He betrayed the Lord for 30 pieces of silver.

While Jesus was praying with His disciples in the Garden of Gethsemane, Judas found his opportunity to betray the Lord. He led the enemy right to Jesus and pointed a finger right at Him:

And while He was still speaking, behold, Judas, one of the twelve, with a great multitude with swords and clubs, came from the chief priests and elders of the people. Now His betrayer had given them a sign, saying, "Whomever I kiss, He is the One; seize Him." Immediately he went up to Jesus and said, "Greetings, Rabbi!" and kissed Him. Jesus replied, "Do what you came for, friend." And suddenly, one of those who were with Jesus stretched out his hand and drew his sword, struck the servant of the high priest, and cut off his ear. But Jesus said to him, "Put your sword in its place, for all who take the sword will perish by the sword (Matthew 26:47-52).

It did not take long for Judas to realize he had made a big mistake. In Matthew 27:3-4 it says:

Then Judas, His betrayer, seeing that He had been condemned, was remorseful and brought back the thirty pieces of silver to the chief priests and elders, saying, "I have sinned by betraying innocent blood."

Notice the motive of his remorse. He knew he had been condemned. He was caught. He was not sorry he betrayed the Lord. He was sorry he was condemned. He tried to give back the money, but the damage was done. He had betrayed the Lord and the wheels of injustice had been set in motion. There was no going back.

At this point, Judas could have repented. He could have asked the Lord's forgiveness for his betrayal, but he did not. Look at his actions, in Matthew 27:5: *Then he threw down the pieces of silver in the temple and departed, and went and hanged himself.*

He threw the money down and committed suicide. There was no repentance. His heart was far from the Lord, but when you look at his life; his heart was never really right with the Lord. The life of Judas was not a life set apart for the Lord. He did not fall into sin when he betrayed the Lord; he never really walked right with the Lord from the beginning.

The Life of Peter—Repentant

Peter was a man who walked closely with the Lord, but he was an impulsive man, so he often said or did the wrong thing. He loved the Lord, but he sometimes allowed his emotions to control him. We see this when Jesus tried to wash his feet, in John 13:8-9:

> *Peter said to Him, "You shall never wash my feet!" Jesus answered him, "If I do not wash you, you have no part with Me." Simon Peter said to Him, "Lord, not my feet only, but also my hands and my head!"*

While Peter's heart was with the Lord, he often acted impulsively and the Lord had to chastise him. Jesus knew Peter's nature and He warned him of his betrayal. He did not speak a parable. He told Peter plainly; you will betray me:

> *Jesus said to him, "Assuredly, I say to you that this night, before the rooster crows, you will deny Me three times." Peter said to Him, "Even if I have to die with You, I will not deny You!" And so said all the disciples* (Matthew 26: 34-35).

It is important to notice, before Jesus warned him, Peter spoke these words in great pride: *Peter answered and said to Him, "Even if all are made to stumble because of You, I will never be made to stumble"* (Matthew 26:33). Again, he was speaking out of emotions. He was not relying on the Lord. He was believing in himself, but his motive was loyalty to the Lord.

In the very same chapter, we see, in spite of Peter's claims, he did betray the Lord (Matthew 26:69-75). Look at how this chapter ends. It tells us:

> *And Peter remembered the word of Jesus who had said to him, "Before the rooster crows, you will deny Me three times." So he went out and wept bitterly* (Matthew 26:75).

Peter wept bitterly. His heart was broken in repentance. He did what he said he would never do; he betrayed the Lord.

This was the difference between Judas and Peter—repentance. God can do amazing things with a repentant heart! Judas committed suicide and Peter went on to see the risen Lord and preach the Gospel of Jesus Christ. Peter was a man with a repentant heart, and God used his life tremendously.

What Leads Us to Repentance?

We have looked at the unrepentant heart and the repentant heart. Many Christians believe we repent when we come to Christ and then we are done, but that is not correct. In order to continue on the path towards the Cross, there must be a continual dying to self and a repentant heart regarding sin.

God leads us to repentance. It is not through our power but through Him. He waits patiently for us, instead of punishing us for our sins. In His patience and goodness towards us, He convicts us of our sins and allows us to see the lost condition of our lives.

While many people think God sends people to hell, it is not the truth. We make the choice with the way we chose to live our lives. God is longsuffering towards man. He gives us many opportunities to come to repentance. Paul said:

> *The coming of the lawless one is according to the working of Satan, with all power, signs, and lying wonders, and with all unrighteous deception among those who perish, because they did not receive the love of the truth, that they might be saved* (2 Thessalonians 2:9-10).

In Romans 2:4, Paul tells us He leads us to repentance in God's goodness:

> *Or do you despise the riches of His goodness, forbearance, and longsuffering, not knowing that the goodness of God leads you to repentance?*

Though the fear of God's wrath may be a motivator for some, in truth, God's goodness causes us to repent. When we understand how much He loves us and how longsuffering He is towards us, it creates a desire to do what is right in His eyes. When you know someone loves you—you have a desire to please them.

God loves us and, in His goodness, He patiently waits for us to turn to Him, but He does not leave us alone. While He is waiting, He is convicting us. He is revealing our true natures to us, so we will recognize our need of a Savior. Acts 2:37 says:

> *Now when they heard this, they were cut to the heart, and said to Peter and the rest of the apostles, "Men and brethren, what shall we do?"*

The word *cut* in the Greek means "to be pricked." God's conviction is like a pricking of the heart. When you feel convicted, you are aware what you are thinking or doing is wrong. It is then you are to act. Notice, in the above Scripture the people were convicted and immediately wanted to act on the conviction.

Repentance is the result of God's longsuffering, goodness and conviction. If you choose to ignore all of these leadings, your heart becomes hard and you become less likely to repent at all. It is not God sending people to hell; you are choosing hell instead of heaven.

Seven Promises of Repentance

Just as the Lord leads and draws us to repentance, He also gives promises to those who repent. Even though He draws us near to

Himself, we still have free will; we can refuse to repent. When we choose to repent, God gives us His promises. In the Scriptures, God has given seven promises to those who repent of their sins and turn to Him.

The first promise we have is forgiveness of sin. In Isaiah 55:7, it says:

> *Let the wicked forsake his way, and the unrighteous man his thoughts; let him return to the Lord, and He will have mercy on him; and to our God, for He will abundantly pardon.*

Second, God promises to be close to the heart of those who repent. Psalm 34:18 says: *The Lord is near to those who have a broken heart, and saves such as have a contrite spirit.*

When we repent of our sins, God hears our prayers and promises He will answer them. He gave this promise to the children of Israel when they were in captivity:

> *When I shut up the heavens so that there is no rain, or command locusts to devour the land or send a plague among my people, if My people who are called by My name will humble themselves, and pray and seek My face, and turn from their wicked ways, then I will hear from heaven, and will forgive their sin and heal their land* (2 Chronicles 7:13-14).

The fourth promise from God is eternal life with Him in heaven. The prophet Ezekiel wrote:

> *"But if a wicked man turns from all his sins which he has committed, keeps all My statutes, and does what is lawful and right, he shall surely live; he shall not die"* (Ezekiel 18:21).

God's fifth promise to the believer is His comfort for their lives. In the Gospel of Matthew, Jesus said: *Blessed are those who mourn, for they shall be comforted* (Matthew 5:4).

God's sixth promise is His Holy Spirit:

> *Then Peter said to them, "Repent, and let every one of you be baptized in the name of Jesus Christ for the remission of sins; and you shall receive the gift of the Holy Spirit"* (Acts 2:38).

For His seventh promise, God will use you as a vessel:

> *Therefore if anyone cleanses himself from the latter, he will be a vessel for honor, sanctified and useful for the Master, prepared for every good work* (2 Timothy 2:21).

God's promises are great and they are guaranteed. God is faithful. No matter how much you have sinned, if you repent, He will bless you and fill you with His peace. Sometimes, He will even spare you some of the consequences of your sins—but sometimes

He will allow you to reap what you sowed, while giving you the strength, the power and the peace to deal with them. Even if He does not alter the consequences, He will work out the situation for good and eventual blessing.

Choosing Repentance

We can look at the consequences of sin and the promises of repentance, but ultimately each person has to make a choice. There is freedom in repentance, as we draw closer to the Lord. With repentance comes the opportunity to be used by the Lord— an opportunity to be a vessel of God.

We do not have to repent, but there are consequences if we do not. With every example in the Bible, the unrepentant heart leads to destruction. While you may not die physically, like Judas, you will have a spiritual death.

If we want to be used by God—servants of the Lord—we must repent and come to Christ, living life with a repentant heart, sensitive to the Holy Spirit. We cannot live according to the world's standards, we have to live according to God's Word, which is what Paul the Apostle taught: *but declared first to those in Damascus and in Jerusalem, and throughout all the region of Judea, and then to the Gentiles, that they should repent, turn to God, and do works befitting repentance* (Acts 26:21).

There is a clear difference between the worldly man's perception of sin and God's perception of sin. The *Moody Monthly Magazine* once printed a version of this poem:

> What is Sin?
> Man calls sin an accident, God calls it an abomination.
> Man calls sin a blunder, God calls it blindness.
> Man calls sin a chance, God calls it a choice.
> Man calls sin a defect, God calls it a disease.
> Man calls sin an error, God calls it enmity.
> Man calls sin fascination, God calls it a fatality.
> Man calls sin infirmity, God calls it iniquity.
> Man calls sin luxury, God calls it lawlessness.
> Man calls sin a trifle, God calls it tragedy.
> Man calls sin a mistake, God calls it madness.
> Man calls sin a weakness, God calls it willfulness.

A man who sees sin as God sees it and has a repentant heart is ready to be used by God.

Chapter 3

The Person God Uses
Lives Under God's Grace

For as by one man's disobedience many were made sinners, so also by one Man's obedience many will be made righteous. Moreover the law entered that the offense might abound. But where sin abounded, grace abounded much more, so that as sin reigned in death, even so grace might reign through righteousness to eternal life through Jesus Christ our Lord.
Romans 5:19-21

Have you ever done something wrong against your spouse or a friend, and instead of receiving their anger and judgment you got a smile and hug? You know you deserved their wrath, but instead, you received unmerited favor. God's grace is like that, it is an amazing thing. In the Bible, the word *grace* is found in the Old Testament and the New Testament. It is *chen* in Hebrew, and it is *charis* in Greek. Whether it is in Greek, Hebrew or English, the word *grace* means "favor, acceptance, good will, loving kindness or reward."

Usually, we receive favor from someone because we have earned it—we have helped them some way. When we receive favor without earning it—or, we receive favor when we deserve punishment—we have received grace. It is favor and acceptance in spite of what we actually deserve. It is a gift.

In the same way, God's salvation and promise of eternal life to you and me is a gift of grace. We do not deserve it—we are sinners. According to God's righteous law, the penalty for sin is death. However, He paid the price for our sins, so we would not have to experience His wrath, but instead experience His loving grace. There is no better illustration of God's grace than the children of Israel—God's chosen people. Look at what Moses said in Deuteronomy 7:6-9:

> *"For you are a holy people to the Lord your God; the Lord your God has chosen you to be a people for Himself, a special treasure above all the peoples on the face of the earth. The Lord did not set His love on you nor choose you because you were more in number than any other people, for you were the least of all peoples; but because the Lord loves you, and because He would keep the oath which He swore to your fathers, the Lord has brought you out with a mighty hand, and redeemed you from the house of bondage, from the hand of Pharaoh king of Egypt. Therefore know that the Lord your God, He is God, the faithful God who keeps covenant and mercy for a thousand generations with those who love Him and keep His commandments"*

As you read the Old Testament, and follow the children of Israel through the years, you see God's unmerited favor time and time again. God did chastise them often, but there was always a remnant of people—God's people—left. In Ezra 9:8, Ezra said:

> *"And now for a little while grace has been shown from the Lord our God, to leave us a remnant to escape, and to give us a peg in His holy place, that our God may enlighten our eyes and give us a measure of revival in our bondage."*

When they sinned against God, He gave them warning after warning before chastising them. In God's judgment, when He brought the Assyrian army against the northern tribes of Israel and the Babylonian army against Judah, God always preserved His remnant:

> *The remnant will return, the remnant of Jacob, to the Mighty God* (Isaiah 10:21).

> *It shall come to pass in that day that the Lord shall set His hand again the second time to recover the remnant of His people who are left, from Assyria and Egypt, from Pathros and Cush, from Elam and Shinar, from Hamath and the islands of the sea* (Isaiah 11:11).

> *"But I will gather the remnant of My flock out of all countries where I have driven them, and bring them back to their folds; and they shall be fruitful and increase"* (Jeremiah 23:3).

Today, we still see God's grace upon His people, as the nation of Israel was re-established May 14, 1948. God brought the Jewish people back to the land He gave to them, and even though they are surrounded by their enemies, God has protected them all these years. Think about it. The children of Israel sinned against the Lord so many times, He had their enemies conquer them and take them away from their land, but in His grace and mercy, He returned them to the land He promised them. The history of the nation of Israel is a true testament to the grace of God, and it is written in God's Word as a lesson to each one of us.

Looking at the history of Israel, we can clearly see, there are no requirements attached to God's grace. You do not have to do 100 good works or say the rosary 500 times, in order to receive His grace. God's grace is a free gift. We did absolutely nothing to deserve God's merit—He chose, by His love, grace and mercy, to save us through the death and resurrection of His Son, Jesus Christ.

Yet, I find it so incredible that people—through their pride and hardness of heart—will say no to God. Do you know how many people I have seen yelling and screaming, cursing at God, while lying in their hospital beds dying? They slip into eternity without accepting God's grace and suffer the tragic consequences.

The Problem with "Good Works"

Have you noticed, over the years the word *sin* has been changed by our society? We have changed the term *homosexuality* to *gay*.

We have changed the sin of *fornication* to a *sexual encounter* and the sin of *adultery* to an *affair*. Our society does not want to call these abominations sin, because they want to accept these things as "alternative lifestyles."

Since our society is changing *sin* to acceptable lifestyles—they are also trying to tell people they can do these sinful acts and still get to heaven. How? Well, as long as you are a good person and do good things, God will accept you. Really? Does the Bible say everyone goes to heaven, as long as they are good? No, I am afraid none of us could ever be good enough, on our own merit, to be accepted by God. Psalm 14:2-3 says:

> *The Lord looks down from heaven upon the children of men, to see if there are any who understand, who seek God. They have all turned aside, they have together become corrupt; there is none who does good, no, not one.*

God's grace and gift of salvation is the only way you and I can enter heaven. The Apostle Paul said:

> *For by grace you have been saved through faith, and that not of yourselves; it is the gift of God, not of works, lest anyone should boast* (Ephesians 2:8-9).

Just imagine; if you and I were able to be saved by our good works, there would be tremendous bragging sessions at church. In fact, we would try to outdo each other, in order to ensure our place in heaven—what a mess that would be. It cannot happen, because mankind is born in sin—and nothing can erase sin but the blood of the Cross. However, most religions teach a salvation by works. Even in biblical times, people were trying to find God's favor by doing good works. It is our natural inclination. Paul said:

> But when the kindness and the love of God our Savior toward man appeared, not by works of righteousness which we have done, but according to His mercy He saved us, through the washing of regeneration and renewing of the Holy Spirit, (Titus 3:4-5).

Not one of us can ever convert anyone to Jesus Christ. It is the Holy Spirit who brings conviction of sin and converts a man's or woman's heart to accept Jesus Christ. Our salvation is based on His grace—what He has already done for us—not what we have done for Him. All we need to do is simply put our faith and trust in Him—He does the rest.

If Christians desire to serve the Lord and be used by God to minister to people, they have to understand grace, because grace reminds us how useless we are without Him. We cannot earn our way to heaven and we cannot spiritually "save" anyone. It is all the work of the Lord. In order to be of use to God, we have to realize how inadequate we really are. We have to be humbled.

A lack of humility is a big reason some people cannot be used by God. There are many people who are hung up on *good works*.

They think they can get to heaven on their own. No matter how many good works you do, it would never be enough to make you righteous. Good works do not set you free from sin. Think of Mother Teresa and all the works she did. She gave her whole life to help and feed the poor in Calcutta. Even though she lived among the poor and did so much to help people, her works would not save her. Her works made her a good humanitarian and showed her compassion, but unless she came to a personal knowledge of the Lord Jesus Christ as Savior of her life, all those great humanitarian works would never get her into heaven. That is what the Bible says. It is only by God's grace we are saved and can enter heaven.

The Law vs. Grace

D.L. Moody once said, "The law brings out sin; grace covers it. The law wounds; the Gospel heals. One is a quiver of arrows; the other a cruise of oil."

Why did God give Moses the Law if the Law could not save people? The Law was a schoolmaster pointing to our sin—it made our conscience guilty and condemned us, because we discovered the behaviors and attitudes we adopted were sinful. Without the Law, we would not understand our guilt. Without the Law, we would not see our need for a Savior. God gave Moses the Law for people to be righteous, but mankind could not keep the Law, because of their sinful nature. The Law was connected to Moses by works, but grace is connected to Jesus Christ through faith. That is the difference. The Law condemned us, but grace frees us. This reminds me of the woman caught in adultery in John 8:2-12:

> *Now early in the morning He came again into the temple, and all the people came to Him; and He sat down and taught them. Then the scribes and Pharisees brought to Him a woman caught in adultery. And when they had set her in the midst, they said to Him, "Teacher, this woman was caught in adultery, in the very act. Now Moses, in the law, commanded us that such should be stoned. But what do You say?" This they said, testing Him, that they might have something of which to accuse Him. But Jesus stooped down and wrote on the ground with His finger, as though He did not hear.*

> *So when they continued asking Him, He raised Himself up and said to them, "He who is without sin among you, let him throw a stone at her first." And again He stooped down and wrote on the ground. Then those who heard it, being convicted by their conscience, went out one by one, beginning with the oldest even to the last. And Jesus was left alone, and the woman standing in the midst. When Jesus had raised Himself up and saw no one but the woman, He said to her, "Woman, where are those accusers of yours? Has no one condemned you?" She said, "No one, Lord." And Jesus said to her, "Neither do I condemn you; go and sin no more."*

According to the Law, the woman, and the man, should have been stoned for adultery. That was the Law—no grace. The scribes and Pharisees were waiting for Jesus to condemn the woman, but

He surprised them. He extended God's grace to her. He knew the people gathered were also sinful and deserved punishment, so He used this opportunity to show them how much grace had been extended to them. They were all sinful, so none of them could throw a stone at her. Just as they could not through a stone, Christ was innocent and could throw the stone, but He chose grace instead. Isn't that beautiful? God's grace!

The Apostle Paul said:

In Him we have redemption through His blood, the forgiveness of sins, according to the riches of His grace which He made to abound toward us in all wisdom and prudence (Ephesians 1:7-8).

When you really experience the grace of God, by placing your faith and trust in Jesus Christ, you are set free from the condemnation of the Law. Something amazing happens—true grace brings forth true works. One day, those works will be examined by God to see what quality they are—gold, silver, wood, hay or stubble. Whatever returns from the fire will be the reward you receive from God. Paul the Apostle explained it to the Corinthian church in 1 Corinthians 3:11-13:

For no other foundation can anyone lay than that which is laid, which is Jesus Christ. Now if anyone builds on this foundation with gold, silver, precious stones, wood, hay, straw, each one's work will become clear; for the Day will declare it, because it will be revealed by fire; and the fire will test each one's work, of what sort it is.

Notice, the foundation for the works we do is Jesus Christ. When God calls us, and we submit to His will, in all humility, recognizing we are saved only by His grace, He will open incredible doors to serve Him. He will work tremendously through our lives to minister to His people and build His Kingdom. It is all about Him, not us.

Chapter 4

The Person God Uses
Has Faith in God

*For I am not ashamed of the gospel of Christ, for it
is the power of God to salvation for everyone who
believes, for the Jew first and also for the Greek.
For in it the righteousness of God is revealed
from faith to faith; as it is written,
"The just shall live by faith."*
Romans 1:16-17

What is faith? William Tyndale, who first translated the Bible into
the English language, said:

"Note now the order: First God gives me light to see the
goodness and righteousness of the law, and mine own sin
and unrighteousness. Out of which knowledge springeth
repentance...Then the same Spirit worketh in mine heart,
trust and confidence to believe the mercy of God and his truth,
that He will do as He hath promised, which belief saveth me."

Paul the Apostle, defined faith in Hebrews 11:1: *Now faith is the substance of things hoped for, the evidence of things not seen.*

Faith is believing what God says—taking Him at His Word—and relying on Him to fulfill His promises for your life. Remember, God has a plan for each one of us and He will take us along the path He has chosen for us, when we put our faith in Him. Then, by faith, we will be used as a servant of the Lord, to build His Kingdom.

If we want to see how God uses people who have put their faith and trust in Him, consider the history of the children of God found in the Book of Hebrews, Chapter 11, the faith chapter:

By faith Abel offered to God a more excellent sacrifice than Cain, through which he obtained witness that he was righteous, God testifying of his gifts; and through it he being dead still speaks.

By faith Enoch was taken away so that he did not see death, "and was not found, because God had taken him"; for before he was taken he had this testimony, that he pleased God. But without faith it is impossible to please Him, for he who comes to God must believe that He is, and that He is a rewarder of those who diligently seek Him.

By faith Noah, being divinely warned of things not yet seen, moved with godly fear, prepared an ark for the saving of his household, by which he condemned the world and became heir of the righteousness which is according to faith.

By faith Abraham obeyed when he was called to go out to the place which he would receive as an inheritance. And he went out, not knowing where he was going. By faith he dwelt in the land of promise as in a foreign country, dwelling in tents with Isaac and Jacob, the heirs with him of the same promise; for he waited for the city which has foundations, whose builder and maker is God.

By faith Sarah herself also received strength to conceive seed, and she bore a child when she was past the age, because she judged Him faithful who had promised. Therefore from one man, and him as good as dead, were born as many as the stars of the sky in multitude—innumerable as the sand which is by the seashore (Hebrews 11:4-12).

Faith is taking God at His Word, knowing and believing; if He said it, He will do it. That is what we see in the lives of all the people in Hebrews 11, men and women who took God on His Word and believed in Him during extreme situations.

Faith is not treating God like your own personal magic genie, like those who follow a trend called positive confession. Those who follow this false doctrine believe God will give them whatever they request—according to their faith, but that concept is wrong. Faith is not about fulfilling your will and your desires—it is about accomplishing God's will in your life. Remember, whenever you pray, it is about believing God will do what is best for your life–He will accomplish His will in and through you.

Faith and the Crippled Man

Do you have to be a super hero of faith in order for the Lord to work in your life? Again, go back and look at the men and women mentioned in Hebrews 11. They were not super stars or super heroes. They were men and women of faith. In Acts 3:1-8, a poor, lame man gives us a great example of faith:

> *Now Peter and John went up together to the temple at the hour of prayer, the ninth hour. And a certain man lame from his mother's womb was carried, whom they laid daily at the gate of the temple which is called Beautiful, to ask alms from those who entered the temple; who, seeing Peter and John about to go into the temple, asked for alms. And fixing his eyes on him, with John, Peter said, "Look at us." So he gave them his attention, expecting to receive something from them. Then Peter said, "Silver and gold I do not have, but what I do have I give you: In the name of Jesus Christ of Nazareth, rise up and walk." And he took him by the right hand and lifted him up, and immediately his feet and ankle bones received strength. So he, leaping up, stood and walked and entered the temple with them—walking, leaping, and praising God.*

Notice, the lame man was in a position of helplessness. Many times, God places us in positions of helplessness, so we have to depend on Him and not our own strength, wisdom and knowledge. At first glance, we would question if "being helpless" is a good thing because in the society we live in, especially in the United States, we are taught self-reliance is the closest thing to godliness.

However, helpless is a good place to be, because it teaches you to trust in the Lord. I believe this is a fundamental act of faith—to trust in the Lord rather than yourself. Our sinful nature, our environment and our culture emphasizes *SELF* as being the master of our lives, instead of God, but in Matthew 16:24, Jesus tells us to deny self—not rely on it. Jesus Christ needs to be Lord of our lives.

When you are in a place of helplessness, God wants your eyes focused on Him, so that you will ask for help and trust He will intervene according to His will. When we are helpless, we submit fully to the Lord, and then He is able to use our lives according to His will and His plan.

The lame man was crippled, which prevented him from functioning in many normal, everyday situations. In the same way, your life can be crippled by sin, which prevents you from functioning in accordance with God's will. Sometimes, the Lord will allow us to encounter difficult situations: financially, emotionally and physically, to get our attention and draw us away from sin and back into fellowship with Him. Sin separates us from God, and, often, when we experience difficulty, we run to the Lord.

The crippled man in Acts 3 did not seek God for healing, but instead relied on other people to help him exist. Peter got to the heart of the problem—getting the lame man to focus on God, to rely on Him rather than others. After he uncovered the root problem, Peter showed the lame man how God could do far more for him than people could. The lame man started out asking for alms from the people passing by, but ended up experiencing the power of God to heal his life.

George Muller said, "Faith does not operate in the realm of the possible. There is no glory for God in that which is humanly possible. Faith begins where man's power ends."

The Object of Your Faith

When Peter saw the needs of the lame man, he challenged him to believe, by faith, in God. The object of your faith is what matters—not faith itself. Stuart Briscoe said, "Faith is only as valid as its object. You could have tremendous faith in very thin ice and drown...you could have very little faith in very thick ice and be perfectly secure."

Peter and John told the crippled man to focus on God and not others. The lame man was healed when he focused on the right object of faith—God.

Though many people say they do not believe in God, they do exercise faith in other objects. They exercise faith when they go to bed at night—they trust their bodies will continue to breathe and function while they sleep. When we get in our cars, we exercise faith to get where we need to go without getting in a car crash. We trust our cars will function properly.

Those who do not believe in God exercise faith when they board the plane—they trust the pilots to fly the plane correctly, to get them to their destination. Even when you are sick, you are exercising faith. You exercise faith when you go to the doctor's office. If he prescribes medicine, you believe the medication is going to make you well.

There is not one single person who does not exercise faith in something on a daily basis. God is concerned about the object of your faith. The Lord does not want you to put your faith in other people, money, possessions or yourself. He wants you to place your faith—your trust and confidence—in Him alone. Without faith in God, the things He calls us to do will seem impossible, but in Matthew 19:26, Jesus said:...*"With men this is impossible, but with God all things are possible."* If our trust is in men, we will never accomplish the impossible. The impossible can only be done through the power of God.

Let's look at the story of Moses and the children of Israel crossing the Red Sea, in Exodus 14. That took tremendous faith:

> *Then Moses stretched out his hand over the sea; and the Lord caused the sea to go back by a strong east wind all that night, and made the sea into dry land, and the waters were divided. So the children of Israel went into the midst of the sea on the*

dry ground, and the waters were a wall to them on their right hand and on their left (Exodus 14:21-22).

Think about what great faith it took for the people to walk into the Red Sea, with the waters piled high on both sides of them. That was not normal. The water could fall down on them at any time. This had never been done before, and they had no idea what to expect, but they took their children, animals and possessions and walked into the midst of the sea. They had faith, not in Moses, but in God. They were trusting God to save them from the Egyptian army.

Salvation is based on the same principles. We need to put our faith and trust in Jesus Christ to save us—He has to be the object of our faith. Only Jesus Christ can forgive us of our sins and give us salvation. Only Jesus Christ can give us eternal life. If the object of our faith is anything other than Jesus Christ—we are still in bondage to sin and separated from God.

Some people put their faith in a religious belief or the church they attend, believing church membership or attending church every Sunday will save their souls. However, the object of their faith is misplaced. The Bible tells us the only person who will save us from our sins is the Lord Jesus Christ:

> *For God did not appoint us to wrath, but to obtain salvation through our Lord Jesus Christ, who died for us, that whether we wake or sleep, we should live together with Him* (1 Thessalonians 5:9-10).

There are many religious groups in the world who put their faith in the wrong object. For example, Muslims put their faith and trust in the Koran and the prophet Muhammad. Idolaters put their trust in graven images to save them. Humanists put their faith in themselves—they are their own god. Philosophers put their faith and trust in ideas and theories. Materialists put their faith and trust in their possessions and money. Religious zealots put their faith and trust in their own good works.

That is not what Jesus taught or what we believe. Just as the children of Israel put their faith in God, Peter offered the lame man the only right object of faith—Jesus Christ.

Walking By Faith

Once we come to Christ, by faith, and receive salvation, we have to continue on in faith. Our need for faith does not end with salvation. It has to be a part of our everyday walk as believers. We have to live our lives trusting in the Lord and the plan He has for our lives, or we will fall back on following our own will, instead of seeking His will.

As we live our lives as Christians, we will need to walk by faith, because without it, we cannot please God. In Hebrews 11:6, Paul the Apostle said:

> *But without faith it is impossible to please Him, for he who comes to God must believe that He is, and that He is a rewarder of those who diligently seek Him.*

No matter how wonderful you are; no matter how many good things you do for other people; no matter how many nights you go to church—you cannot please the Lord unless you have faith in Him. The closer you draw to God the greater your faith will be. Your heart and thoughts become, "I am His, and He is mine, and I trust Him with my whole life."

As we grow in our knowledge of God, through His Word, our faith will grow. Romans 10:17 says: *So then faith comes by hearing, and hearing by the word of God.* Every time you hear the Word of God taught, and every time you read the Bible, you are building your faith. The Scriptures teach us, exhort us, correct us, inspire us and encourage us. The more we know the Bible, the greater our faith will be.

When we build upon the Word of God, we have a defense against the enemy. We will all face the wiles of Satan and his demons, but we do not have to worry, because faith is our defensive weapon against them. Ephesians 6:16 says: *above all, taking the shield of faith with which you will be able to quench all the fiery darts of the wicked one.* The only way Satan can touch a Christian is by God's permission. The Lord is in control of your life, not the enemy. Your faith nullifies the devil's darts, because everything he does is based on lies. If you have faith in the Lord and His Word, you can resist Satan's accusations and lies.

God's Word tells us true faith brings true works in the life of every believer. Without faith, we will not have true works of the Lord.

James and Paul were in agreement with each other, because Paul said we are saved through faith in God: *For by grace you have been saved through faith, and that not of yourselves; it is the gift of God,* (Ephesians 2:8), and James said true faith brings forth true works: *Thus also faith by itself, if it does not have works, is dead* (James 2:17). The heart of God is to serve others. When you have real faith in your life, you have a desire to help others and to further the Kingdom of God by serving the Lord with your talents and skills.

It is only through faith we will have victory over this world. John the Beloved said: *For whatever is born of God overcomes the world. And this is the victory that has overcome the world—our faith* (1 John 5:4). Your faith and my faith in God make us overcome this world. When you watch the news and get upset about what is happening in our country and in the world, take heart—your faith is greater than the evil in the world. God is in control and knows every detail—He will take care of you.

Faith is a way of a life for a Christian. Paul the Apostle said: *For in it the righteousness of God is revealed from faith to faith; as it is written, "The just shall live by faith."* (Romans 1:17). You must rely on God to meet your needs and to take care of you on a daily basis. You can count on His promises for a hopeful future, and believe in His Word that you will never die but live eternally with Him in heaven. Faith in Jesus Christ is our motivator and sustainer to live each day with joy, peace and hope. Without faith, our lives would be in shambles.

Similarly, Paul told the church in Corinth, followers of Christ walk by faith: *For we walk by faith, not by sight* (2 Corinthians 5:7). If we could see everything before it happened, we would not need faith.

In the Old Testament, God promised Abraham he would have a child and the child would be the father of a great nation (Genesis 17). Many years went by without the promise being fulfilled. When Abraham was 100 years old, and Sarah was 90, God told them they would have a baby (Genesis 18). Sarah laughed at God, but she became pregnant and had Isaac (Genesis 21). Abraham believed God, even when he could not see how the promise would be fulfilled.

Nothing is impossible to God—you need to walk by faith—in other words live day to day expecting God to fulfill His promises and to take care of you. Do not despair, because you are focused on your situations or circumstances.

Praying by Faith

As Christians, faith is fundamental to our spiritual walk with the Lord. It is only by faith we can walk and live by faith, but even greater, it is only by faith we can enter into prayer with the Lord. It takes faith to pray. In Matthew 21:21-22:

> *…Jesus answered and said to them, "Assuredly, I say to you, if you have faith and do not doubt, you will not only do what was done to the fig tree, but also if you say to this*

mountain, 'Be removed and be cast into the sea,' it will be done. And whatever things you ask in prayer, believing, you will receive."

When you pray, you are trusting God to hear your prayer and to answer it according to His will.

Prayer is your communication with God, and if you do not have faith in the Lord you will never pray to Him. There are many people who repeat vain prayers to unknown gods or saints but have no faith in the objects of their prayers. Prayer for them is a ritual.

However, as believers, prayer is not a ritual but a vital link to the Lord of our life. A relationship without communication is not a close relationship at all. The Lord wants to be close to you—the only way you can draw near to God is by talking to Him. Faith plays a vital role in your prayer life.

Grow in Faith

Clearly faith is important for the believer in every area of their life, from believing in God to trusting He is faithful in His promises and will answer our prayers. Without faith, we will not have a spiritual walk with the Lord.

Do you take God at His Word? Is your faith great or small? Even in the midst of a dark storm, when you cannot see the way, you can have faith God will lead you safely through. It is through faith in

Jesus Christ, we will grow closer to the Lord and He will be able to use our lives to serve in His purposes and plans.

> *"For I through the law died to the law that I might live to God. I have been crucified with Christ; it is no longer I who live, but Christ lives in me; and the life which I now live in the flesh I live by faith in the Son of God, who loved me and gave Himself for me. I do not set aside the grace of God; for if righteousness comes through the law, then Christ died in vain"* (Galatians 2:19-21).

Chapter 5

The Person God Uses
Counts the Cost

And whoever does not bear his cross and come after
Me cannot be My disciple. For which of you, intending
to build a tower, does not sit down first and count the cost,
whether he has enough to finish it— lest, after he has
laid the foundation, and is not able to finish, all
who see it begin to mock him.
Luke 14:27-29

Once, when I taught a leadership class, I challenged the students to do something I had tried myself. I told them to take seven pieces of paper, one for each day of the week, and write down what they did every half-hour, from the moment they got up to the moment they went to bed. At the end of the week, I told them to add up the amount of time they spent on themselves and the amount of time they spent on the things of God.

Can you imagine what they learned through that activity? I was surprised to see how much time I wasted on dumb things! How many times do we say to ourselves, "I did not have time to read my Bible today," or "I just do not have the time to pray in the morning before going to work"?

I challenge you to do the same exercise. You may be very surprised at how much time you spend on yourself and how little time you spend on the things that matter to God.

If you want to really know what it means to count the cost and sacrifice your life for the Lord, look at the life of Paul the Apostle. He was a man who was fully committed to serving the Lord, without compromise.

In 2 Corinthians, Paul wrote to the Corinthian church about the false prophets with their false teachings. He was concerned about their spiritual lives and wanted them to know what a true disciple of Christ looked like. He said this about his life in the Lord:

> *Are they Hebrews? So am I. Are they Israelites? So am I. Are they the seed of Abraham? So am I. Are they ministers of Christ?—I speak as a fool—I am more: in labors more abundant, in stripes above measure, in prisons more frequently, in deaths often. From the Jews five times I received forty stripes minus one. Three times I was beaten with rods; once I was stoned; three times I was shipwrecked; a night and a day I have been in the deep; in journeys often, in perils of*

waters, in perils of robbers, in perils of my own countrymen, in perils of the Gentiles, in perils in the city, in perils in the wilderness, in perils in the sea, in perils among false brethren; in weariness and toil, in sleeplessness often, in hunger and thirst, in fastings often, in cold and nakedness—besides the other things, what comes upon me daily: my deep concern for all the churches. Who is weak, and I am not weak? Who is made to stumble, and I do not burn with indignation? If I must boast, I will boast in the things which concern my infirmity (2 Corinthians 11:22-30).

Paul was called by the Lord to bring the Gospel of Jesus Christ to the Gentiles. He suffered greatly, but his love for God and his love for the people was greater than the infirmities he suffered. He truly counted the cost.

The Cost of Discipleship

Jesus did not play games with people. He did not promise His disciples a luxurious life of wealth, health and happiness, which, unfortunately, some ministers teach today. Instead, Jesus told them there was a cost to following Him. In Mark 8:34-38 He said:

When He had called the people to Himself, with His disciples also, He said to them, "Whoever desires to come after Me, let him deny himself, and take up his cross, and follow Me. For whoever desires to save his life will lose it, but whoever loses his life for My sake and the gospel's will save it. For what will it profit a man if he gains the whole world, and loses his own soul? Or what will a man give in exchange for his soul? For whoever is ashamed of Me and My words in this adulterous and sinful generation, of him the Son of Man also will be ashamed when He comes in the glory of His Father with the holy angels."

Jesus Christ challenged His disciples to count the cost of discipleship. Now, before you think, *Well, I am not a disciple—I am just an ordinary Christian,* let me explain what it means to be a disciple.

In the New Testament, in the Greek language, *disciple* means "learner." Accepting Jesus Christ as your Lord and Savior does not just mean coming to the front of the church to make a public declaration—it means becoming a disciple, or learner, of Jesus Christ. Discipleship is not about joining a church or attending church services. It is about giving your will and your life to God, taking upon yourself the responsibility of touching other people's lives for Jesus Christ, just as God touched yours.

Do you love the Lord enough to be His disciple? Are you willing to sacrifice your own life to serve God?

God promised an abundant life but not a carefree and luxurious life. If you were to listen to some of the "faith" teachers'—prosperity doctrine—you would be told the opposite. They teach that Christians are to be healthy and wealthy. If you are sick or have a disease, it is because you lack faith. If you are poor or driving a clunker car, it is because you lack faith.

According to these false teachers, there is no cost to discipleship. In fact, they act as if God owes us something. How absurd!

In fact, Jesus Christ owned nothing and experienced many diverse trials. His life was not safe, luxurious and carefree, but it was abundantly joyful, fruitful and purposeful.

As Christians, we are all disciples of Christ; now we have to look at what Christ said to His disciples and how they needed to count the cost—how we need to count the cost as we follow Him.

Deny Yourself

The first requirement of a disciple can be found in the first part of Mark 8:34 where Jesus states: *"Whoever desires to come after Me, let him deny himself, ..."* While the secular world tells us to *indulge ourselves*, Jesus Christ tells us to *deny ourselves*. We have a picture of self-denial compared to self-indulgence in Luke 21, with the story of the widow's mite:

> *And He looked up and saw the rich putting their gifts into the treasury, and He saw also a certain poor widow putting in two mites. So He said, "Truly I say to you that this poor widow has put in more than all; for all these out of their abundance have put in offerings for God, but she out of her poverty put in all the livelihood that she had"* (Luke 21:1-3).

While the widow denied her own needs to give to the Lord, the rich people gave what they could easily afford and did it for all the people to see. In their abundance, they did not deny any of their desires.

We were all very much like the rich people before we came to Christ. Think about your life before Christ. You called your own shots and did whatever you wanted to do—*self* was on the throne. You indulged your fleshly appetites without giving any regard to the things of God.

When you came to Jesus Christ, you realized your mind, body and soul belonged to God. Suddenly, it was no longer you who lived but Christ who lived in you (Galatians 2:20). Instead of being *self-centered*, a disciple of Christ becomes *Christ-centered*. Your focus is no longer on you but on God and others.

One of the greatest hindrances in the Christian life is self. It is in complete opposition to the teachings of Christ, because everything He did was for us.

Unfortunately, selfishness is a characteristic of our sinful human nature. In Galatians 5:19-21, Paul wrote about our selfish nature:

> *Now the works of the flesh are evident, which are: adultery, fornication, uncleanness, lewdness, idolatry, sorcery, hatred, contentions, jealousies, outbursts of wrath, selfish ambitions, dissensions, heresies, envy, murders, drunkenness, revelries, and the like; of which I tell you beforehand, just as I also told*

you in time past, that those who practice such things will not inherit the kingdom of God.

As Christians, we are called to be Christ-like and self-centeredness is not part of a Christ-like character. Paul pointed out our need to deny our selfish nature and become more like Christ when he wrote to the church in Colosse:

Therefore, as the elect of God, holy and beloved, put on tender mercies, kindness, humility, meekness, longsuffering; bearing with one another, and forgiving one another, if anyone has a complaint against another; even as Christ forgave you, so you also must do (Colossians 3:12-13).

The only way we can truly deny ourselves and become more like Christ is through repentance. Because self-centeredness is a sin, it requires repentance, so we can be empowered by the Holy Spirit to overcome it.

Have mercy upon me, O God, according to Your lovingkindness; according to the multitude of Your tender mercies, blot out my transgressions. Wash me thoroughly from my iniquity, and cleanse me from my sin (Psalm 51:1-2).

If we decide to live our lives selfishly, we will be the first ones to suffer the consequences, as it hinders our ability to love others. In Romans 12:9, Paul said: *Let love be without hypocrisy. Abhor what is evil. Cling to what is good.* Then, in 1 Corinthians 13:4-5, he said: *Love suffers long and is kind; …does not seek its own.*

Even after we come to Christ, our sinful, selfish nature will continue to battle God for control over our lives. That is why we must learn to do as Paul told the Romans:

> *I beseech you therefore, brethren, by the mercies of God, that you present your bodies a living sacrifice, holy, acceptable to God, which is your reasonable service. And do not be conformed to this world, but be transformed by the renewing of your mind, that you may prove what is that good and acceptable and perfect will of God* (Romans 12:1-2).

That is what discipleship entails—a dying to ourselves and a commitment to follow Jesus Christ no matter what the cost may be.

Take Up Your Cross

After Jesus told His disciples to deny themselves, He then said, *and take up his cross* (Mark 8:34). I find this very interesting. Jesus told them this prior to His own crucifixion. In yet another way, the Lord revealed what would happen to Him, and how He would fulfill prophecy. What does it mean to *take up your cross*?

It is important to know what the Cross of Jesus Christ represents. The Cross is an instrument of suffering and death. The Roman Empire put people to death by crucifying them on crosses. It was the most horrible death a person could ever experience.

Caesar Nero, who killed Paul the Apostle, crucified Christians by hanging them on crosses, putting tar on them and lighting them like torches, while he circled them in his chariot. He also crucified and burned thousands along the highway to Rome.

The cross represents torture and death. The Cross of Christ represents selflessly and willingly enduring torture and death. Are you willing to identify yourself with Jesus Christ in this way? Are you willing to *take up your cross* by dying to self and enduring suffering as a part of God's plan for your life?

John Gregory Mantle said, "There is a great difference between realizing, 'On that Cross He was crucified for me,' and 'On that Cross I am crucified with Him.' The one aspect brings us deliverance from sin's condemnation, the other from sin's power."

Follow Him

Jesus Christ calls us to: *"...follow Me"* (Mark 8:34), without any hesitation or excuse. Notice, He put this requirement of discipleship after denying ourselves and taking up our crosses. This is certainly not a coincidence. The Lord knows in order to follow Him completely, people must die to self and be willing to identify and bear the suffering of the Cross.

When Jesus calls you and anoints you to serve and follow Him, there has to be a radical change in your life. You no longer live for yourself, but you live for Christ. This mindset is in complete opposition to our true nature, which is inherently selfish.

When Jesus called His disciples to follow Him, they all left various lifestyles to do so. In the same way, when you commit to following Christ, you will see a radical change in your life—including the way you think, the way you act, the way you speak and the things you do.

Making the decision to follow Christ is a conscious decision. You do not just fall into following Jesus. You choose to follow Him, knowing the cost, just as the disciples made a conscious decision to follow the Lord. They were not in a hypnotic trance, but freely chose to commit their lives to Jesus.

The Lord does not want a robot—He wants you to intelligently look at who He is and what He has done for you, so you can make a conscious decision to follow Him.

For those who know and love you, your decision to follow Christ will seem like a radical commitment—and it is. The Lord did not ask for a partial commitment but an all-encompassing, radical commitment. He expects us to give up ownership of our lives and give Him complete authority. Radical commitment means putting Christ first in all we do and never turning back—even when faced with martyrdom.

Choose—Hot or Cold

Today, many people walk the fence between following Christ and following the world. In fact, many are walking away from the Lord and completely selling out to the world. In the end, they cannot be used by the Lord, and they lose their lives eternally. In the Book of Revelation, Jesus said:

> *"I know your works, that you are neither cold nor hot. I could wish you were cold or hot. So then, because you are lukewarm, and neither cold nor hot, I will vomit you out of My mouth. Because you say, 'I am rich, have become wealthy, and have need of nothing'—and do not know that you are wretched, miserable, poor, blind, and naked"* (Revelation 3:15-17).

Knowing the end for those who compromise, how important is it to be a millionaire, a superstar, an athlete or even the most knowledgeable person in the world when it all comes to eternity?

Following Christ and the world do not coincide. Following Jesus Christ is a full-time effort—a complete and whole commitment. That is why it is so important to understand what Christ desires from your life. Jesus said: *"For whoever desires to save his life will lose it, but whoever loses his life for My sake will find it"* (Matthew 16:25).

As followers of Christ, we have the greatest blessing. We get to be used by God. He has entrusted us with the Gospel of Jesus Christ, which has the power to save people eternally.

Paul the Apostle suffered greatly as he took the Gospel to the Gentile nations, but in the end, he believed his suffering was of no account. He counted the cost and knew reaching people with the love and hope of the Gospel message was greater than his own comfort—greater even than his own life. It is evident in his last words to Timothy:

> *Therefore do not be ashamed of the testimony of our Lord, nor of me His prisoner, but share with me in the sufferings for the gospel according to the power of God, who has saved us and called us with a holy calling, not according to our works, but according to His own purpose and grace which was given to us in Christ Jesus before time began, but has now been revealed by the appearing of our Savior Jesus Christ, who has abolished death and brought life and immortality to light through the gospel, to which I was appointed a preacher, an apostle, and a teacher of the Gentiles. For this reason I also suffer these things; nevertheless I am not ashamed, for I know whom I have believed and am persuaded that He is able to keep what I have committed to Him until that Day* (2 Timothy 1:8-12).

Chapter 6

The Person God Uses
Knows the Holy Spirit

And being assembled together with them, He commanded
them not to depart from Jerusalem, but to wait for the
Promise of the Father, "which," He said, "you have
heard from Me; for John truly baptized with water,
but you shall be baptized with the Holy Spirit
not many days from now."
Acts 1:4-5

When Jesus left this earth, He knew the disciples would experience great opposition and persecution. Before He went to the Cross, He told them: *I will not leave you orphans; I will come to you* (John 14:18). He knew they would need spiritual support once He ascended, or they would not be spiritually equipped to do the work He called them to do.

Christ called the disciples to preach the Gospel to the world, and then He spiritually equipped them for the calling. The Holy Spirit was sent to empower them for their calling. Without the work of the Holy Spirit, the world would never have heard the Gospel of Jesus Christ. While Christ sent the disciples out, the Holy Spirit empowered them to do the work.

What Christ did for the disciples, He will do for you and me. Before the Lord can use our lives, we have to be empowered by the Holy Spirit. We cannot just know about Him, we have to be filled with and empowered by Him. Without Him, it is impossible for us to fulfill the call of Christ in our lives. We can try doing it in our own power, but we will fail. It is a spiritual call and must be done in spiritual power.

Today, many people say they want to be used by God, but they do not really have the capacity to stand for Jesus Christ. In John 14, Jesus was on His way to the Cross. On His way, He knew He had to tell His disciples about the Holy Spirit. In the Book of John, Chapters 12 through 17 are the last days of Jesus on the earth, right before His crucifixion. Jesus had been with His disciples for three and a half years and it was time for Him to tell them about the Holy Spirit, so they would not become discouraged. He reassured them:

> *"If you love Me, keep My commandments. And I will pray the Father, and He will give you another Helper, that He may abide with you forever—the Spirit of truth, whom the world cannot receive, because it neither sees Him nor knows Him; but you know Him, for He dwells with you and will be in you. I will not leave you orphans; I will come to you"* (John 14:15-18).

Jesus was facing the last week of His life. He had told the disciples He was going to die; rise three days later and ascend to heaven. The disciples did not really believe Jesus was going to die. Yet, the Lord kept preparing them for His death—promising them He would not leave them as orphans but would send the Holy Spirit to help and comfort them.

The Character and Work of the Holy Spirit

The Holy Spirit is not an essence but an actual person. He is the third person of the Godhead—the Trinity—with attributes of God. Before we come to Christ, He brings conviction to our lives, drawing us to Jesus. When we give our lives to Christ, He comes in and dwells within us. Then, He comes upon us, to empower us for the work of the ministry.

While all Christians receive the *with* and *in* experience of the Holy Spirit, not all Christians have the *upon* experience. Without the *upon* experience, we are not equipped for the calling of God in our lives. The work of God must be done through the power of God—the empowering of the Holy Spirit.

As One of the Trinity, the Holy Spirit has the same attributes of God. He is omniscient, knowing everything, from beginning to the end; omnipresent, in all places at one time; and omnipotent, all powerful.

The Holy Spirit calls and equips us for the ministry, by His very nature. He is aware of everything happening in our lives and in the world and has a specific plan for your life and my life. He calls you to the time and place He has for you. In Acts 13:2, He called out Saul and Barnabas: *As they ministered to the Lord and fasted, the Holy Spirit said, "Now separate to Me Barnabas and Saul for the work to which I have called them."*

As He calls and equips us, He gives spiritual gifts to each one of us separately, as He wills, according to our call. It is not our will; it is the mind and the will of God. Paul the Apostle explained this in 1 Corinthians 12:11: *But one and the same Spirit works all these things, distributing to each one individually as He wills.*

One way the Holy Spirit helps us, as we serve Him, is to bring God's Word to our memories. John 14:26 says:

> *"But the Helper, the Holy Spirit, whom the Father will send in My name, He will teach you all things, and bring to your remembrance all things that I said to you."*

Keep in mind; the only things He can bring to your remembrance are the things you have read and studied. If you have never read the Old Testament, then nothing from the Old Testament will ever be given to you.

That is why it is so important to read through the Bible—line upon line, precept upon precept—to obtain the full counsel of God. The Holy Spirit has a wonderful way of bringing up the Scriptures you need at just the right time, whether to minister to you or for you to minster to others.

The Holy Spirit brings moral conviction to our lives. This is evident in Acts 5:3:

> *But Peter said, "Ananias, why has Satan filled your heart to lie to the Holy Spirit and keep back part of the price of the land for yourself?"*

The Holy Spirit convicts us of our sins today, as well, but mercifully, we do not drop dead like Ananias and Sapphira. Instead, the moment you lie or cheat, the Holy Spirit is there to tell you "do not do that."

Like us, the Holy Spirit also has emotions. Paul revealed the heart of the Holy Spirit in his writings to the churches:

> *Now I beg you, brethren, through the Lord Jesus Christ, and through the love of the Spirit, that you strive together with me in prayers to God for me* (Romans 15:30).

> *And do not grieve the Holy Spirit of God, by whom you were sealed for the day of redemption* (Ephesians 4:30).

In both of these Scriptures, the Holy Spirit displays very powerful emotions. He both *loves* and *grieves*. Since the Holy Spirit is a person—He manifests emotions just as you and I do. In the New Testament the word *grieve* in the Greek language is "to bring pain." The Holy Spirit gets hurt when you sin. As a Christian, He resides in your heart and is a part of your life—so when you tell a lie, commit adultery, cheat a friend or hate another human being, you are directly offending and hurting the Spirit of God residing in you.

Have you ever been at a loss for words when it comes to prayer? Have you ever felt so distraught you simply did not know what to pray? The Holy Spirit knows what is going on in your life, and He intercedes for you and for me. In Romans 8:27, Paul said:

> *Now He who searches the hearts knows what the mind of the Spirit is, because He makes intercession for the saints according to the will of God.*

He knows what is on your mind and in your heart. There are times when all we can do is groan and the Holy Spirit comes alongside us and intercedes on our behalf in prayer. Everything the Spirit does is in accordance with God's will. When we are distressed, the Holy Spirit prays for us according to the Lord's will for our lives.

Before we come to Christ and give our life to Him, the Holy Spirit calls us to God. Revelation 22:17 says: *And the Spirit and the bride say, "Come!" And let him who hears say, "Come!"*...Do you remember when the Holy Spirit called you to salvation?

I remember the night I gave my life to the Lord, very clearly. I was frustrated, empty and angry. My wife was at the end of her rope— she was going to take our kids and leave me. Filled with rage and despair, I got my rifle and waited for them to come home.

As I waited, I hit the television with my rifle and it turned on to Chuck Smith preaching. I watched him smile and talk about the love of God. It was like he had a bow and arrow and was shooting me in the heart. His words brought conviction to my heart. I know now it was the Holy Spirit working on me. I fell to my knees sobbing, asking God to forgive me for all I had done.

It took some time for my wife, Sharon, to believe I was really changed, but through the work of the Holy Spirit, she saw the changes and the fruit of His work in me. All these years later, I am teaching the Word of God and sharing the Gospel at church and on the airwaves.

The Holy Spirit is the only one who can call us, and He is the only one who can draw us to salvation. My life is a living testament of this truth.

False Teaching about the Holy Spirit

While the Bible clearly teaches the truth about the nature of the Holy Spirit, false teaching about the Holy Spirit has become almost common place. All you have to do is attend certain charismatic churches; turn on the television; or read specific books on the subject, and you will see mass confusion and sometimes downright nonsense.

In 1994, there was a movement in Canada called the Toronto Blessing. People claimed the Holy Spirit was upon them, making them bark like dogs, roar like lions, talk like babies, shake and quake and laugh uncontrollably.

Unbelievably, this movement spread like wildfire throughout the United States, as well. The leaders and individuals who propagated this false doctrine said it was "evidence" of the Holy Spirit at work. They did not know the true nature of the Holy Spirit.

Nowhere in Scripture does the Holy Spirit tell us to behave like an animal or to lose control. The Bible tells us the opposite—the Holy Spirit works in an orderly fashion and promotes self-control (1 Corinthians 14:40). We need to understand; emotional experiences must be backed up by Scripture.

Those who follow these false doctrines may not know the Holy Spirit and chance not being used by God. It may appear like they are doing great things for the Lord, but because all the attention is on them and not the Lord; we know it is not a work of the Lord.

When God uses our lives, He gets all the glory. If you are taking the glory, you are not walking in the Spirit; you are walking in the flesh.

Jesus warned us, in the Last Days there would be a great deception in the church orchestrated by demons: *For false christs and false prophets will rise and show great signs and wonders to deceive, if possible, even the elect* (Matthew 24:24).

Paul the Apostle later went on to warn us in 1 Timothy 4:1: *Now the Spirit expressly says that in latter times some will depart from the faith, giving heed to deceiving spirits and doctrines of demons.*

This is not the time to fall asleep and be deceived by false teachers and false doctrines. If we heed the prompting of the Holy Spirit in our lives, we will not fall away, but we have to know Him, so we can identify the devil and his demons disguised as angels, to deceive us.

> "A man full of the Spirit is one who is living a normal Christian life. Fullness of the Spirit is not the state of spiritual aristocracy, to which only a few can attain."
> —G. Campbell Morgan

Chapter 7

The Person God Uses
Has a Prayer Life

*"Watch and pray, lest you enter into temptation. The spirit
indeed is willing, but the flesh is weak."*
Matthew 26:41

With these few words, Jesus spelled out the very necessity for
prayer in the lives of Christians. Without prayer and communion
with the Lord, we are in danger of falling into temptation. There
is so much power in prayer, without it, we cannot be used by God.
If we do not spend time in prayer and in God's Word, we cannot
possibly know the call God has for each one of us, individually.

If we read the Old Testament, there is recorded history of the
many people God used, and they were all men and women of
prayer. Look at the life of Nehemiah. He was in captivity in Persia,
when he got word from his brother of the conditions in Jerusalem.
Before speaking to anyone about the problems, Nehemiah went
before the Lord in prayer:

> *So it was, when I heard these words, that I sat down and wept, and mourned for many days; I was fasting and praying before the God of heaven. And I said: "I pray, Lord God of heaven, O great and awesome God, You who keep Your covenant and mercy with those who love You and observe Your commandments, please let Your ear be attentive and Your eyes open, that You may hear the prayer of Your servant which I pray before You now, day and night, for the children of Israel Your servants, and confess the sins of the children of Israel which we have sinned against You. Both my father's house and I have sinned"* (Nehemiah 1:4-6).

Nehemiah knew only the Lord could take care of problems in Jerusalem. Prayer was not his last resort, it was his strongest weapon. He wanted the Lord to use him in Jerusalem, but he had to get there first. He trusted the Lord to empower him and go before him, so he prayed for God's intervention.

There is nothing more powerful than a man or woman on their knees before God. William Cowper said, "Satan trembles when he sees the weakest saint upon his knees."

Imagine the difference in our homes, places of work, communities and our world, if each of us spent at least 15 minutes in conference with God every day. I believe broken homes would be mended, temptations resisted, anger subsided and compassion extended.

Prayer is so powerful—and important—but so few Christians spend time doing it. Many Christians try to take care of things on their own or go to friends for assistance. When all else fails, they turn to God in prayer. Let's learn from Nehemiah; prayer should be our first resort and mightiest weapon.

The Object of Our Prayers

Webster's dictionary defines *prayer*: "To offer devout petition, praise, and thanksgiving to God or to an object of worship." The object of worship—the person you are praying to is of key importance when it comes to answered prayer. The Hare Krishna's pray to Krishna and the Muslims pray to Allah, but all prayers are not equal, because of the recipient of the prayer, not the person praying.

There is a great deception in the world today. People believe all roads lead to God, no matter what you do. In fact, there are interfaith groups trying to bring Buddhists, Hindus, Muslims, Catholics and Protestants together as one greater church body. In essence, they are saying it does not matter what god you worship—all roads lead to God.

There is only one road leading to God: *Because narrow is the gate and difficult is the way which leads to life, and there are few who find it* (Matthew 7:14). The Bible says the only people who will ever see God are those who have a personal relationship with Jesus Christ—period.

Acts 4:12 says: *Nor is there salvation in any other, for there is no other name under heaven given among men by which we must be saved."*

There is only One, True, Living God, so the only prayers heard are those addressed to the Lord God. Jesus Christ died on the Cross to be the mediator between man and God. You do not need to address prayers to anyone other than Jesus. If you do, they will go unheard. The object of your worship must be Jesus Christ, in order for God to hear your prayer.

Do We Really Have to Pray?

The Bible says it is a sin not to pray to God: *Moreover, as for me, far be it from me that I should sin against the Lord in ceasing to pray for you; but I will teach you the good and the right way* (1 Samuel 12:23). No matter how often you go to church or read your Bible, if you are not praying to the Lord, you are sinning against Him. I think many Christians feel prayer is an elective instead of a required course.

Martin Luther said: "To be a Christian without prayer is no more possible than to be alive without oxygen." Think about that for a moment. Without oxygen we cannot live. We would die. The same thing holds true for a person who is not in prayer before God. Slowly but surely the person dies spiritually. Though it is a sin not to pray, we should be motivated to pray because we want to stay in close communication with the Lord.

John Bunyan often said, "Sin will keep a man from prayer, or prayer will keep a man from sin." How true. When someone stops praying and seeking God, their flesh takes over their lives and they are living as an unbeliever, a carnal Christian, rather than a child of God.

God desires you would seek Him. First Chronicles 16:11 says: *Seek the Lord and His strength; seek His face evermore!* As a Christian, if you stop talking to God, you are not going to have a close and vital relationship with Him—it is as simple as that.

If you are living a life of sin, God does not listen to your prayers. Remember, sin separates us from God. Isaiah the prophet said: *But your iniquities have separated you from your God; and your sins have hidden His face from you, so that He will not hear* (Isaiah 59:2). A sinful lifestyle cuts off communication to God.

There is a time when the Lord hears the prayer of a sinner—when he is confessing his sin and repenting of it, but He will not hear the prayer of man or woman who is continuing in sin, not confessing it or turning from it.

Misconceptions of Prayer

There are several beliefs people have about prayer, which are not biblical. It is important to know what the Bible teaches about prayer, or you could be deceived. You may find yourself practicing man-made traditions instead of heartfelt communication with the Lord.

The first thing you want to look at is your motive. Are you treating God like your magic genie, praying to Him for all your wants and desires or are you truly seeking to know Him and His will for your life? This is the "name it and claim it" doctrine. Are you praying from the heart or praying to get things from the Lord? They support their false doctrine with these verses in Luke 11:9-10:

> *"So I say to you, ask, and it will be given to you; seek, and you will find; knock, and it will be opened to you. For everyone who asks receives, and he who seeks finds, and to him who knocks it will be opened."*

While it is true, God wants to bless us, everything is done according to His will, not our own. He knows the things that will destroy us and will not give those things to us. Those who profess the "name it and claim it" doctrine completely ignore this verse in 1 John 5:14: *Now this is the confidence that we have in Him, that if we ask anything according to His will, He hears us.*

Prayer should always be pure in motive—desiring to draw closer to God; to know His will for your life; and to intercede on behalf of others.

Another common misconception about prayer is the vain repetitious prayers encouraged by some denominations. Jesus, Himself, said: *"And when you pray, do not use vain repetitions as the heathen do. For they think that they will be heard for their many words"* (Matthew 6:7).

Notice, repetitious prayers were something the heathens did to their false gods who could not hear them. God wants us to speak to Him from our hearts. As a child, I was taught to pray by repetition. Think about how God feels when people pray like a robot—10 Hail Mary's and 10 Our Father's.

How would you feel if your family or friends spoke to you that way? There is no real communication when you use vain repetitions. God wants you to talk to Him as you would your closest friend. He wants you to speak from the heart.

Posture of Prayer

We have to remember; when we pray, we are coming before a holy God. As we enter into prayer, we need pure hearts. This does not mean we are perfect but we are forgiven because we have sought forgiveness from the Lord. We have a pure heart, not a perfect heart. The psalmist wrote: *If I regard iniquity in my heart, the Lord will not hear. But certainly God has heard me; He has attended to the voice of my prayer* (Psalm 66:18-19). As long as you have a sinful heart, God cannot hear you until you repent.

Along with a pure heart, we need to have contrite hearts. A contrite heart is a penitent heart—one sincerely sorry and desirous to make things right. Psalm 51:17 says: *The sacrifices of God are a broken spirit, a broken and a contrite heart—these, O God, You will not despise.* The Lord will not listen to the prayers of the unrepentant—but someone truly broken over their sin will be heard by God.

Again, we have another heart condition. When we come before the Lord, we need humble hearts. Jesus told a parable about a Pharisee and a repentant sinner:

"Two men went up to the temple to pray, one a Pharisee and the other a tax collector. The Pharisee stood and prayed thus with himself, 'God, I thank You that I am not like other men—extortioners, unjust, adulterers, or even as this tax collector. I fast twice a week; I give tithes of all that I possess.' And the tax collector, standing afar off, would not so much as raise his eyes to heaven, but beat his breast, saying, 'God, be merciful to me a sinner!' I tell you, this man went down to his house justified rather than the other; for everyone who exalts himself will be humbled, and he who humbles himself will be exalted." (Luke 18:10-14).

God hates pride. It was the downfall of Lucifer and for many men and women. The arrogance of man is sheer foolishness to God. Jesus said: *And whoever exalts himself will be humbled, and he who humbles himself will be exalted* (Matthew 23:12). God will abase the proud man, but He will exalt the humble man.

The Lord has forgiven us of our sins, so if we want to be heard when we come before Him, we need a forgiving spirit. When you forgive someone, you are giving up your right to retaliate. Since God has forgiven you of your many sins, you must forgive those who have hurt you as well. In Matthew 6:14-15, Jesus said:

"For if you forgive men their trespasses, your heavenly Father will also forgive you. But if you do not forgive men their trespasses, neither will your Father forgive your trespasses."

Many times, when we pray, we are asking the Lord to do something or provide something we want, which is not wrong, but we should always ask according to God's will, not our will. Jesus taught us to seek God's will in Luke 11:2:

> So He said to them, "When you pray, say: Our Father in heaven, Hallowed be Your name. Your kingdom come. Your will be done On earth as it is in heaven."

Prayer is not a means to get your will done, but to find out what God's will is for your life. Often, people will ask God for things that are not in accordance to His will, and then they wonder why He is not helping them.

When we come to the Lord in prayer, He already knows our needs. Matthew 6:8 says: *"Therefore do not be like them. For your Father knows the things you have need of before you ask Him."* If God knows what I need, then why pray? The Lord wants you to rely on Him for your needs. He wants your faith and trust in Him to be complete. When you come to Him with your spiritual, emotional and physical needs, it shows you are seeking His provision rather than relying on your own abilities and schemes. Prayer increases our reliance on God.

As I look back over my life, I am glad the Lord did not give me everything I prayed for. He knows best, and if you are truly interested in doing what God wants you to do, He will reveal His will to you in prayer.

When we come before the Lord in prayer, we need to come with a thankful heart. Philippians 4:6 says this:

> *Be anxious for nothing, but in everything by prayer and supplication, with thanksgiving, let your requests be made known to God;...*

If you wrote down all the blessings in your life, you would be surprised just how much God takes care of you. Do you have a roof over your head? Do you have food in the refrigerator? Be thankful. God loves a grateful heart—not a grumbling, murmuring heart.

When you pray with the right heart, the right motive and the right attitude, your prayers actually rise to heaven. Revelation 8:3-4 says:

> *Then another angel, having a golden censer, came and stood at the altar. He was given much incense, that he should offer it with the prayers of all the saints upon the golden altar which was before the throne. And the smoke of the incense, with the prayers of the saints, ascended before God from the angel's hand.*

What a picture! An angel carrying a censor with all of the prayers of the saints before the throne of God, where he opens the censor and the prayers begin to float out into the presence of God. Some of those prayers are yours and some are mine.

God's Faithful to Hear Us

God is so faithful. When we come before Him in prayer, He hears us and He is faithful to answer. The prophet Isaiah had this message from the Lord:

> *"Go and tell Hezekiah, 'Thus says the Lord, the God of David your father: "I have heard your prayer, I have seen your tears; surely I will add to your days fifteen years"'"* (Isaiah 38:5).

Many times, your prayer will be answered instantly, like Hezekiah, sometimes in a couple of hours, sometimes a couple of days, sometimes weeks, months, years, and sometimes your prayer will be answered after you die. God answers prayer in His perfect timing, but be assured, your prayers are not bouncing off the walls. They are in the very presence of God.

All through the Old Testament, we see God's people sin and suffer the consequences of their sin. Then when they repented before the Lord, He heard and answered their prayers. They went back and forth, going into captivity and then being delivered from captivity.

Every time they walked away from the Lord, God still heard their prayers and restored them when they cried out to Him. Look at these verses:

...if My people who are called by My name will humble themselves, and pray and seek My face, and turn from their wicked ways, then I will hear from heaven, and will forgive their sin and heal their land (2 Chronicles 7:14).

Therefore You delivered them into the hand of their enemies, who oppressed them; and in the time of their trouble, when they cried to You, You heard from heaven; and according to Your abundant mercies You gave them deliverers who saved them from the hand of their enemies (Nehemiah 9:27).

Then you will call upon Me and go and pray to Me, and I will listen to you. And you will seek Me and find Me, when you search for Me with all your heart. I will be found by you, says the Lord, "and I will bring you back from your captivity; I will gather you from all the nations and from all the places where I have driven you," says the Lord," and I will bring you to the place from which I cause you to be carried away captive" (Jeremiah 29:12-14).

God is so faithful. When we come to Him in prayer and supplication, He hears us and He responds. We can be like the children of Israel, walking with God and then walking away from Him, or we can walk with Him consistently, in prayer.

If we choose to walk in close communion with the Lord, He will hear us and He will use our lives, blessing us and the people we come in contact with. Paul the Apostle exhorted Timothy to be a man of prayer, and he exhorts us still today:

Therefore I exhort first of all that supplications, prayers, intercessions, and giving of thanks be made for all men, for kings and all who are in authority, that we may lead a quiet and peaceable life in all godliness and reverence. For this is good and acceptable in the sight of God our Savior (1 Timothy 2:1-3).

Chapter 8

The Person God Uses
Studies God's Word

For the word of God is living and powerful, and sharper than any two-edged sword, piercing even to the division of soul and spirit, and of joints and marrow, and is a discerner of the thoughts and intents of the heart.

Hebrews 4:12

The power of the Word of God is miraculous. The Bible tells us it is living, powerful and sharper than any two-edged sword. The Word of God discerns the thoughts and intents of the heart. This all seems impossible. How can the Bible be living? How does it know our thoughts and intents?

John the Beloved gave us the answer: *In the beginning was the Word, and the Word was with God, and the Word was God* (John 1:1). The Word was from the beginning, which is in reference to Jesus Christ. The Word is transforming because it is the transforming work of Jesus Christ.

As a believer and a servant of the Lord, we have to know God's Word, because only then do we know God. It is through His Word we know Him; and we have something of value to give to others.

I will never forget the time I was humiliated by one of my professors at the university I was attending. I was taking a hermeneutics class, which is a class about biblical interpretation. One particular assignment was to pick a passage of a book we were studying in seminary and interpret it, without the aid of biblical commentaries.

I picked the Book of Amos, specifically, the passage speaking of the "cows of Bashan." After turning in my paper, the professor asked the class, "Who are the cows of Bashan?" Since I had been studying the Scriptures for a long time, I confidently raised my hand and told him, "The cows of Bashan were prostitutes." My professor, went to the blackboard and wrote, "Stupid." He then said, "Mr. Ries, I want you to go home, read the text and then come back next week and tell me who the cows of Bashan are."

I had been taught the cows of Bashan were prostitutes. I had even read it in many commentaries, so I went home and read the Book of Amos and studied the text. When I came to the fourth chapter of the Book of Amos, I read the true answer:

> *Hear this word, you cows of Bashan, who are on the mountain of Samaria, who oppress the poor, who crush the needy, who say to your husbands, "Bring wine, let us drink!"* (Amos 4:1).

The Scriptures clearly show the cows of Bashan were rich, fat women who were oppressing the poor.

I learned a big lesson that day—I need to know the Word of God; I need to study God's Word, especially before I speak.

No one who is a believer can live without the Word of God in their lives. Job 23:12 says: *I have not departed from the commandment of His lips; I have treasured the words of His mouth more than my necessary food.*

Job said it is more important to feed on the Word of God each day than it is to eat three square meals. Why? Through His Word, God can minister to us, no matter what is happening in our lives. He has the answer; He provides peace and comfort.

I found this poem years ago, written anonymously, and it really points out how God's Word is necessary for every person to be spiritually stable:

Who Should Read the Bible?

The young—to learn how to live
The old—to know how to die
The ignorant—for wisdom
The learned—for humility
The rich—for compassion
The poor—for comfort
The dreamer—for enchantment

The practical—for counsel
The weak—for strength
The strong—for direction
The haughty—for warning
The humble—for exaltation
The troubled—for peace
The weary—for rest
The sinner—for salvation
The doubting—for assurance
All Christians—for guidance

Puritan pastor, Thomas Brooks said this about the power and influence of the Word of God:

"The Word of the Lord is a light to guide you, a counselor to counsel you, a comfort to comfort you, a staff to support you, a sword to defend you, and a physician to cure you. The Word is a mine to enrich you, a robe to clothe you, and a crown to crown you."

Different Titles of the Bible

If we are going to study God's Word and share it with others, we have to be aware of the various titles used in reference to the Bible. There are different ways the writers of God's Word spoke of it. In the Old Testament, you will find it referred to as *The Law* most often. Psalm 1:2 says: *But his delight is in the law of the Lord, and in His law he meditates day and night.*

The children of Israel were given the Ten Commandments as a means of a law to live by. The Book of Leviticus clearly lists the details of the law, which the people were to follow. The law was everything to Israel. Through it, they discovered God's will for their lives.

However, they also discovered it was impossible for them to keep it. That is why Jesus Christ came to earth—to save us from the penalty of the law and to be the righteousness of the law fulfilled. Only Christ could keep God's law perfectly—and through His blood, we also are considered "righteous."

Second reference to the Bible is *The Scriptures*, which is found in Romans 1:2: *which He promised before through His prophets in the Holy Scriptures.* Notice, the Scriptures are holy. As God spoke to men, they wrote down what was dictated to them by the Holy Spirit. Written originally in Hebrew, Aramaic and Greek, the Scriptures are without error, directly inspired by God.

The promise referred to is Jesus Christ. John wrote: *You search the Scriptures, for in them you think you have eternal life; and these are they which testify of Me* (John 5:39). The Scriptures reveal the plan of salvation through Jesus Christ. They clearly teach Jesus Christ is the Messiah, the long-awaited redeemer of mankind.

Third, is very similar to the Scriptures. We saw in the Scriptures, the Bible is the inspired Word of God, so we will see it referred to as *the Word of God* or *Word of the Lord.*

The psalmist wrote: *As for God, His way is perfect; the word of the Lord is proven; He is a shield to all who trust in Him* (Psalm 18:30). Then, 2 Peter 3:5 says:

> *For this they willfully forget: that by the word of God the heavens were of old, and the earth standing out of water and in the water.*

The Bible is God's Word to mankind. It shows His will for your life—to be saved, to follow Him and give Him glory. The Word of God is not only to be learned but is a call to action. James 1:21-23 says:

> *Therefore lay aside all filthiness and overflow of wickedness, and receive with meekness the implanted word, which is able to save your souls. But be doers of the word, and not hearers only, deceiving yourselves. For if anyone is a hearer of the word and not a doer, he is like a man observing his natural face in a mirror.*

Paul told the Philippian church: *holding fast the word of life, so that I may rejoice in the day of Christ that I have not run in vain or labored in vain* (Philippians 2:16). The Bible is *The Word of Life,* as God's Word gives life—both on earth and eternally—to all those who believe it and follow it.

It does not matter which title you use in reference to the Bible. What is important to know is its transforming power. When you apply the Bible to your life, you will experience God's will—the abundant life Jesus Christ spoke about to His disciples.

The Bible's Power to Transform

The Book of Acts tells us Paul made three missionary journeys. He brought the Gospel message to many people in many countries, and used the Word of God to teach, preach, exhort and transform lives. After leaving the church in Thessalonica, Paul went on to Berea:

> *These were more fair-minded than those in Thessalonica, in that they received the word with all readiness, and searched the Scriptures daily to find out whether these things were so. Therefore many of them believed, and also not a few of the Greeks, prominent women as well as men* (Acts 17:11-12).

Notice, the people searched the Scriptures and believed. The Word of God transformed their lives. Why does the Bible have the power to transform lives? It reveals the living God to us. I am always amazed at how many people come up to me and say, "I want to know God," but they have never bothered to read His words.

In Luke 24:6-7, we read the account of the two angels who were outside of Jesus' tomb. When the women came to the tomb, the angels said to them:

> *"He is not here, but is risen! Remember how He spoke to you when He was still in Galilee, saying, 'The Son of Man must be delivered into the hands of sinful men, and be crucified, and the third day rise again.'"*

Throughout the Old Testament and the New Testament, the message of the Gospel is clear—Jesus Christ is the promised Messiah and the Son of God. From Genesis to Revelation, the Bible reveals the Jesus Christ, our Savior and Redeemer; the One who transforms lives, giving us a future and a hope. This very message brings the powerful transformation to our lives—leading us out of darkness and into the light of God's kingdom.

The Roadmap to Life

If we truly want to be servants of the Lord, we have to know God's Word and believe it is without error, the very words of God. It is only through the Scriptures we can learn of the character and nature of God—enabling us to know Him and His plan of salvation.

The Bible also helps believers follow and choose the right path for their lives. In a sense, the Word of God is our "owner's manual" for life. Psalm 119:19 says: *I am a stranger in the earth; do not hide Your commandments from me.*

God is not in the business of hiding anything from us. In fact, He desires we come to Him in prayer, and study His Word for counsel. As we travel through life, the Bible should be our road map, pointing out safe routes, obstacles to avoid and our final destination. If we choose to ignore God's Word, we will wander aimlessly through life and risk missing our real destination.

The Word of God is everything to a servant of the Lord. It is our guide; our power; our inspiration; our biography of God; our hope; and it is reveals our future.

If we want the Word of God to affect our lives, we need to know and understand the Bible is pure: *The statutes of the Lord are right, rejoicing the heart; the commandment of the Lord is pure, enlightening the eyes* (Psalm 19:8); restraining: *Your word I have hidden in my heart, that I might not sin against You* (Psalm 119:11); perfect: *The law of the Lord is perfect, converting the soul; the testimony of the Lord is sure, making wise the simple* (Psalm 19:7); true: *Your righteousness is an everlasting righteousness, and Your law is truth* (Psalm 119:142); enduring: *"The grass withers, the flower fades, but the word of our God stands forever"* (Isaiah 40:8); effectual: *So shall My word be that goes forth from My mouth; it shall not return to Me void, but it shall accomplish what I please, and it shall prosper in the thing for which I sent it* (Isaiah 55:11); and inspired: *So Moses came and called for the elders of the people, and laid before them all these words which the Lord commanded him* (Exodus 19:7).

Without God's Word living in our hearts and minds, we are of no use to the Lord or to others. If we give people anything other than God's Word, we have given them nothing of worth—nothing lasting.

When we study and know God's Word, we will be armed with the greatest weapon and defense we could ever imagine.

Paul the Apostle lists the Bible as one piece of our spiritual armor: *...the sword of the Spirit, which is the word of God*(Ephesians 6:16) and again in Hebrews 4:12: *For the word of God is living and powerful, and sharper than any two-edged sword.*

While all things die and pass away, the Word of God, this powerful sword, will last forever. First Peter 1:25 tells us: *But the word of the LORD endures forever.*

Chapter 9

The Person God Uses
Loves & Forgives

Bless the Lord, O my soul, and forget not all His benefits:
who forgives all your iniquities, who heals all your diseases,
who redeems your life from destruction, who crowns you
with lovingkindness and tender mercies,
Psalms 103:2-4

King David was a man who was intimately acquainted with the love and forgiveness of God. While he was a man after God's heart and walked with the Lord, he fell in sexual sin, tried to cover it up with murder, and in spite of his great sin, still experienced the love and forgiveness of the Lord. That is why he was able to write Psalm 103. He truly knew the forgiveness of God that comes from His lovingkindness.

When we read the Word of God, love and forgiveness are so closely linked. We see them in action time and time again, through the works of the Lord, but to truly understand how to love and forgive others, we have to look at godly love and godly forgiveness, individually.

Godly Love vs. the Love of the World

Love is powerful. Yet, in today's world, *love* is often a hurtful, selfish and lustful action. The love of this world does not come close to the love of the Lord and the love He wants us to have for others. Paul the Apostle gives us great insight into the true meaning of love in his first letter to the Corinthian church:

> *Love suffers long and is kind; love does not envy; love does not parade itself, is not puffed up; does not behave rudely, does not seek its own, is not provoked, thinks no evil; does not rejoice in iniquity, but rejoices in the truth; bears all things, believes all things, hopes all things, endures all things. Love never fails. But whether there are prophecies, they will fail; whether there are tongues, they will cease; whether there is knowledge, it will vanish away* (1 Corinthians 13:4-8).

Just think how different our world would be if we all loved each other like this. The Apostle Paul clearly shows us how to love people in the above Scripture.

Paul was not the first person in the Bible to teach about godly love. He learned about it from studying the Old Testament. In the Book of Leviticus, God tells us how to treat people:

> *You shall not take vengeance, nor bear any grudge against the children of your people, but you shall love your neighbor as yourself: I am the Lord* (Leviticus 19:18).

In other words, you need to treat people the way you want to be treated. Notice, love and forgiveness are together in this command, for we cannot truly love others if we do not forgive them or bear grudges against them.

Our society confuses love and lust. God's love is unselfish. It thinks about the other person and acts accordingly. There is no room for selfishness in true love. If we are honest, we will admit this kind of love, as Paul defined it, goes against our natural tendencies. The only way we can give love, without expecting something in return, is through the help of the Holy Spirit. Only God can give us the ability to love according to His standards.

We see the true love and forgiveness of the Lord displayed in a man when we look at the life and death of Stephen:

> *When they heard these things they were cut to the heart, and they gnashed at him with their teeth. But he, being full of the Holy Spirit, gazed into heaven and saw the glory of God, and Jesus standing at the right hand of God, and said, "Look! I see the heavens opened and the Son of Man standing at the right hand of God!"*
>
> *Then they cried out with a loud voice, stopped their ears, and ran at him with one accord; and they cast him out of the city and stoned him. And the witnesses laid down their clothes at the feet of a young man named Saul. And they stoned Stephen as he was calling on God and saying, "Lord Jesus, receive my*

spirit." Then he knelt down and cried out with a loud voice,
"Lord, do not charge them with this sin." And when he had
said this, he fell asleep (Acts 7:54-60).

When the people were stoning Stephen, he prayed for God to forgive them for murdering him. It is hard to imagine, but notice, it says he was full of the Holy Spirit. It was the work of the Lord, enabling him to love and forgive the people who were stoning him. In our fleshly nature, it is impossible for us to love and forgive our enemies.

Biblical Guidelines for Human Love

If we are going to call ourselves Christians and ask the Lord to use our lives, we have to have godly love—love for God and love for others. It may seem hard, even impossible, but the Bible gives us clear instruction on godly love and what God expects.

First, we must realize love is a spiritual gift and it is more important than any other spiritual gifts. If we want to display godly love, we have to ask the Holy Spirit to give it to us and we have to value it above any other gift. Paul told the Corinthians:

Though I speak with the tongues of men and of angels, but
have not love, I have become sounding brass or a clanging
cymbal. And though I have the gift of prophecy, and
understand all mysteries and all knowledge, and though
I have all faith, so that I could remove mountains, but have
not love, I am nothing. And though I bestow all my goods

to feed the poor, and though I give my body to be burned, but have not love, it profits me nothing (1 Corinthians 13:1-3).

The Apostle Paul made it clear to the church. Love is far more important than the spiritual gifts you use. In fact, if you are using your spiritual gifts without a heart of love for others, they are useless to God. Love makes our actions and gifts useful. Although people have different gifts, love is available to everyone.

As servants of the Lord, love is not optional; it is a command. John wrote:

Again, a new commandment I write to you, which thing is true in Him and in you, because the darkness is passing away, and the true light is already shining. He who says he is in the light, and hates his brother, is in darkness until now. He who loves his brother abides in the light, and there is no cause for stumbling in him (1 John 2:8-10).

In the church, love is expressed through self-sacrifice and servanthood. In fact, we are to reach out in love beyond our friends to our enemies and persecutors as well.

Love should be the very thing unifying the church; it should be the Christian's birth mark—identifying to the world we are Christians. Love is the key to walking in the light, because we cannot grow in love if we hate other people.

While we are commanded to love others throughout the Scriptures, it is not automatic. God does not force us to love others. We have to choose to love others. The Bible says:

> *And let us consider one another in order to stir up love and good works, not forsaking the assembling of ourselves together, as is the manner of some, but exhorting one another, and so much the more as you see the Day approaching* (Hebrews 10:24-25).

This may seem like a shock to you, but love is not merely a feeling, but a choice. We can choose to be concerned with other people's well-being and treat them with respect and kindness whether we feel like it or not. We can choose to show love to people we do not like. Every day, you and I are given opportunities to love people—if we choose to love, God will help us express our love.

Clearly, it is easier to love our friends than our enemies. However, the love God wants us to show one another extends to our enemies and those we simply do not like. In Luke 6:27-28, Jesus says:

> *"But I say to you who hear: Love your enemies, do good to those who hate you, bless those who curse you, and pray for those who spitefully use you."*

If we only love our friends and family what kind of love would that be? Jesus went on to say: *"But if you love those who love you, what credit is that to you? For even sinners love those who love them"* (Luke 6:32).

The love of God extends to everyone—especially sinners. Remember, the Bible tells us we will be known by our love. If we only love our friends, we are no different than the non-believer, who does not have the love of the Lord.

Loving God while Loving People

If you love God you will love people, but if you hate people it is impossible for you to love God. John wrote this:

If someone says, "I love God," and hates his brother, he is a liar; for he who does not love his brother whom he has seen, how can he love God whom he has not seen? (1 John 4:20).

Jesus was a loving man. He loved everyone—especially sinners. He loved His enemies. His love for others was the best example we could ever have. As the people persecuted Him and sought to kill Him, He loved them. He loved them, and He loves us, all the way to the Cross.

According to Jesus, God's laws can be reduced to two simple principles: love God and love others.

Jesus answered him, "The first of all the commandments is: 'Hear, O Israel, the Lord our God, the Lord is one. And you shall love the Lord your God with all your heart, with all your soul, with all your mind, and with all your strength.' This is the first commandment. And the second, like it, is this:

'You shall love your neighbor as yourself.' There is no other commandment greater than these" (Mark 12:29-31).

When you love God completely and care for others as you care for yourself, then you have fulfilled the intent of the Ten Commandments and the other Old Testament laws.

If you love God and you love others as you love yourself, you will not lie to them, hurt them, abuse them, steal from them, rape or murder them; you also, will not take another person's wife or husband and commit adultery.

In reality, the nature of all crime is a lack of love for God and people. That is why the further our country gets away from God, the more immoral and dangerous it becomes. People cannot keep the Ten Commandments on their own merit. In fact, none of us can love others the way we are supposed to unless we have the love of God in our heart. The foundational principle to loving people is to first love God.

Unlimited Forgiveness

Just as Jesus is the ultimate example of unconditional love, His life displays forgiveness as only God can forgive. In His unlimited grace and mercy, God pours out His love and forgiveness on our lives, and He calls us to love and forgive others.

When Jesus was teaching the disciples how to pray with the model prayer, He said this: *And forgive us our debts, as we forgive our debtors*

(Matthew 6:12). God has forgiven us our sins, Jesus took them to the Cross with Him, so how can we bear a grudge and not forgive others?

Everyone has been or will be hurt by another person at some point in their life. It is not so much how you are hurt but how you deal with it that counts. When you refuse to forgive someone who has hurt you—you are the one who suffers in the long run. Bearing grudges and bitterness causes physical, emotional and spiritual problems.

I have learned over the years, I cannot hold a grudge, because it literally eats me up. It consumes my mind and my heart and destroys my relationship with the Lord.

Many people say, "Well, I will forgive them this time, but that is it. They better not do anything else!" Honestly, is that the attitude of someone who has a forgiving spirit? If God treated us the same way—we would all be in trouble. How many times are you supposed to forgive someone? Is there a limit to forgiveness? In the Book of Matthew, Jesus said:

> *Then Peter came to Him and said, "Lord, how often shall my brother sin against me, and I forgive him? Up to seven times?" Jesus said to him, "I do not say to you, up to seven times, but up to seventy times seven"* (Matthew 18:21-22).

Peter, like most of us, felt seven times was more than a gracious amount to forgive somebody, but the Lord told him, and is telling us, forgiveness should be unlimited. This is reasonable when you consider His forgiveness for us is unlimited. God's forgiveness for us puts everything in perspective.

It is terrible when you see angry people—people who hold on to bitterness and refuse to forgive. They are hard, unbearable and critical in their demeanor. Jesus was very clear—we need to forgive at all times.

Now let me clarify something—to forgive someone does not mean we need to keep enduring their abuse or treatment. Once I forgive them, it does not mean I have to have fellowship with them. They can go their way, and I can go my way, but I have to make sure my heart is right before the Lord. That is what God desires.

When you forgive someone, you are not saying their behavior is correct, and they can keep treating you poorly, but you are saying you relinquish your right to get even or to judge them. What matters is that your heart is right before God—you have forgiven those who have hurt you, just as God has forgiven you for the sins you have committed against Him.

We Forgive Others Because God Has Forgiven Us!

Too often, we want God to have mercy on us—to forgive us of all our sins and stupidity—but we want His judgment and wrath to rain down on those who have done evil against us. What is the basis for us to forgive others? Simple, we forgive those who trespass against us, because God forgives our trespasses. In fact, God said if we do not forgive others He will not forgive us:

"For if you forgive men their trespasses, your heavenly Father will also forgive you. But if you do not forgive men their trespasses, neither will your Father forgive your trespasses" (Matthew 6:14-15).

In the Book of Matthew, Jesus told a parable to illustrate the importance of forgiveness:

"Therefore the kingdom of heaven is like a certain king who wanted to settle accounts with his servants. And when he had begun to settle accounts, one was brought to him who owed him ten thousand talents. But as he was not able to pay, his master commanded that he be sold, with his wife and children and all that he had, and that payment be made. The servant therefore fell down before him, saying, 'Master, have patience with me, and I will pay you all.' Then the master of that servant was moved with compassion, released him, and forgave him the debt. "But that servant went out and found one of his fellow servants who owed him a hundred denarii; and he laid hands on him and took him by the throat, saying, 'Pay me what you owe!' So his fellow servant fell down at his feet and begged him, saying, 'Have patience with me, and I will pay you all.' And he would not, but went and threw him into prison till he should pay the debt. So when his fellow servants saw what had been done, they were very grieved, and came and told their master all that had been done. Then his master, after he had called him, said to him, 'You wicked servant! I forgave you all that debt because you begged me.

*Should you not also have had compassion on your fellow
servant, just as I had pity on you?' And his master was angry,
and delivered him to the torturers until he should pay all that
was due to him. "So My heavenly Father also will do to you
if each of you, from his heart, does not forgive his brother his
trespasses."* (Matthew 18:23-35).

When we read the above passage, we understand how evil it was
for this guy to hassle the person who owed him a few dollars when
he had been forgiven a debt of several thousands.

In the same way, God is disgusted when we hold onto to an offense
and refuse to forgive when He gave His very life to forgive us our
sins. The debts we have against God are huge compared to the
offenses done to us by other people—no matter how grievous those
offenses may seem.

When you refuse to forgive someone, you are essentially slapping
the Lord in the face, saying, "My sins are not that bad. You did not
have to die on the Cross for me!"

No matter how *good* you may think you are, in reality you are a
sinner deserving of hell. It is only by God's grace and mercy—by
the blood of the Cross—you are made clean and whole in God's
eyes. Jesus assumed your penalty for sin, and through His gift of
salvation, we are considered righteous. If God sacrificed His Son,
so you could have a relationship with Him and join Him in heaven,
then how can you refuse to forgive others for their petty offenses?

If you have bitterness in your heart—if you are holding onto a grudge—get rid of it now. Forgive those who have offended you, just as Christ forgave you your many debts. You will find your life will be far more joyous and peaceful when you extend forgiveness to others. Most importantly, as you forgive others, God will also forgive you and use your life tremendously.

Love and Forgiveness Hand in Hand

When we think of the love of the Lord, we cannot fail to also think of His forgiveness. Surely, we do not deserve either, but in His great grace and mercy, He pours out His love upon us and forgives us, just as He loved and forgave the sinful woman in Luke 7:44-49:

Then He turned to the woman and said to Simon, "Do you see this woman? I entered your house; you gave Me no water for My feet, but she has washed My feet with her tears and wiped them with the hair of her head. You gave Me no kiss, but this woman has not ceased to kiss My feet since the time I came in. You did not anoint My head with oil, but this woman has anointed My feet with fragrant oil. Therefore I say to you, her sins, which are many, are forgiven, for she loved much. But to whom little is forgiven, the same loves little." Then He said to her, "Your sins are forgiven." And those who sat at the table with Him began to say to themselves, "Who is this who even forgives sins?" Then He said to the woman, "Your faith has saved you. Go in peace."

Now that you know the true love and forgiveness of God, you have to establish them in your own life, so you can be used as servant of the Lord. Without these two key elements in our lives, there is no way the Lord can use us. When we portray love and forgiveness to others, they will see the Lord in our lives, as it is only through He empowering we can truly love and forgive, not our friends and family, but strangers and enemies.

Chapter 10

The Person God Uses
Understands Physical & Spiritual Death

We are confident, yes, well pleased rather to be absent from the body and to be present with the Lord.
2 Corinthians 5:8

Paul the Apostle understood death and did not fear it. He told the Corinthian church, when we leave our physical bodies in death, we will be with the Lord. We may die physically but our spirits are eternal. Before we enter eternity, we will choose whether we will be with Christ in heaven and live or go to hell and die spiritually.

Today, our culture does everything it can to avoid age and death. We are focused on the physical body. Youth and vitality are the gods of this world, and people will go to great lengths to stay "young." Plastic surgery procedures and medical science continually try to provide the "fountain of youth."

Here is a news flash—we are all going to die. Our physical bodies will perish in the end. The Bible says: *And as it is appointed for men to die once, but after this the judgment,* (Hebrews 9:27); yet, most people, especially young people, do not wake up thinking, *Maybe I am going to die today.*

The truth is, many people believe they are going to physically live forever. They believe death only happens to other people, but the Bible says no one escapes death—everyone will die. You do not have to be 90 to die; you can die, any time between birth and old age. Death can come knocking at your door any time.

Lazarus and the Rich Man

People say: "I want to go to heaven. I want to see God," and yet they do not want to die. Many people believe they will go to heaven, but they have never repented and accepted Jesus as their Lord and Savior. They do not understand death or eternity.

While the idea of heaven is very popular, the concept of hell makes people uncomfortable. They do not want to go to hell, so they just dismiss the whole concept of it.

However, hell is a very real place, and if it is not dealt with here on earth, people will deal with it in eternity. In Luke 16, the Bible tells a true story regarding heaven and hell with a rich man and Lazarus, a beggar.

The rich man had everything in life money could buy. He spent his time drinking, eating and being merry, you might say he was a "partier." Then there was Lazarus, who had nothing. His life was a stark contrast to the rich man. Lazarus walked the streets of Jerusalem, going through the trash cans for something to eat. He was homeless and hungry every day.

One day, Lazarus came to the rich man's mansion and sat at the gate. While a party took place inside, Lazarus waited, along with the dogs, for the crumbs of food falling from the table. As the poor beggar put the crumbs in his mouth, the dogs would lick the sores covering his body.

As the evening wore on, the poor man died. Immediately, the angels came to take his spirit to Abraham's Bosom, a compartment in hell for the righteous, where he would be comforted. Since Christ had not yet come to set the captives free, everyone who died went to hell. There were two compartments in hell, one for the righteous and one for the wicked, with a great gulf separating the two.

That same evening, the rich man also died, but angels did not come to take his spirit to the compartment for the righteous. Instead, he experienced the torment of fire in hell, the compartment reserved for the wicked. Since he rejected the love and grace of God while he lived, he was tormented continually in hell, and he still possessed all five senses.

The rich man looked across the gulf and saw Lazarus being comforted by Abraham. Notice, on earth he did not know Lazarus, but in hell he knew him by name and he knew Abraham. The rich man called out:

> *"Father Abraham, have mercy on me, and send Lazarus that he may dip the tip of his finger in water and cool my tongue; for I am tormented in this flame"* (Luke 16:24).

The rich man wanted the same comfort he had while he was living.

> *But Abraham said, 'Son, remember that in your lifetime you received your good things, and likewise Lazarus evil things; but now he is comforted and you are tormented. And besides all this, between us and you there is a great gulf fixed, so that those who want to pass from here to you cannot, nor can those from there pass to us'* (Luke 16:25-26).

The rich man had given no attention to eternal life—to God's grace—while he was living—now, the party was over. There was nothing he could do.

This is a lesson to each one of us. If you continue to reject God's grace in your lifetime, there will come a day when it is too late to receive God's mercy.

We have to make the choice while we are living—live like the rich man or like Lazarus. If you know God's grace and have accepted

Jesus Christ as your Savior, you have a glorious future. No matter how difficult your life may be right now—the Lord is faithful and will keep His promise to you. Be encouraged—you have a future and a hope.

If you have decided to eat, drink and be merry because you believe life is too short not to enjoy; then enjoy all your pleasures right here on earth, but remember you will be tormented in eternity. We make the choice and it has to be made now, for once death comes, it will be too late.

False Beliefs about Death

There are many false beliefs about death, because there are so many false beliefs about life and man's final destination. The largest breeding grounds for false beliefs are in our universities and colleges throughout the nation. They are predominantly populated with liberal, atheistic professors, who teach their liberal philosophies, which remove God from the picture. Paul the Apostle warned about "vain philosophies" and those who would teach them:

> *Beware lest anyone cheat you through philosophy and empty deceit, according to the tradition of men, according to the basic principles of the world, and not according to Christ* (Colossians 2:8).

Whether it is the liberal elite, the intellectuals of our day, or the artistic community—these people are atheistic. They believe in evolution and offer strange theories regarding death.

Some people believe you cease to exist when you die. That is it. Since they do not believe there is eternal life, they live for the moment, without a moral compass.

Then there are those who believe in reincarnation; when you die you come back to life as an animal or another person. Many Hindu people in India are starving, because they refuse to eat cows; fearing one of them may be a relative. Once again, the wrong belief about death controls how they live.

Finally, there are people who believe everyone goes to heaven when you die, but it is a false heaven. In their heaven, every desire is fulfilled. This belief has become widespread in America, but it is dangerous, because it teaches God is love and leaves out His wrath. God's Word tells us there will be an accounting. Read the Book of Revelation and you will learn of the wrath of God.

It is false to believe all roads lead to heaven. It does not matter which god you believe in, we are all going to end up in a "good place" because God would never send anybody to hell. This is a belief that does not even recognize hell.

I find it interesting, as people approach death, their false beliefs often crumble. I have seen it first hand as I have visited nursing homes. Those who come to the end of their lives without the Lord are tormented, even before they die. Consider the lives of these two famous atheists:

"Writers H.G. Wells and George Bernard Shaw were brilliant men, yet they rejected the message of Scripture. They placed their trust in their own systems of belief, which were based on human reason. Yet, they could not find lasting inner peace, and they slowly lost confidence in what they believed. Wells' final literary work, for example, has been aptly called a 'scream of despair.' And shortly before Shaw died in 1950 he wrote, 'The science to which I pinned my faith is bankrupt...its counsels, which should have established the millennium, have led directly to the suicide of Europe. I believed them once... in their name I helped to destroy the faith of millions... And now they look at me and witness the great tragedy of an atheist who has lost his faith.'"

The Truth About Death

God made mankind in His own image. We are different from any other living being because we possess a soul and a spirit. The Apostle Paul said in 1 Thessalonians 5:23:

Now may the God of peace Himself sanctify you completely; and may your whole spirit, soul, and body be preserved blameless at the coming of our Lord Jesus Christ.

When God created man, He formed him from the dust in the ground. In other words, we are made of dirt. Just as we were formed of dust—we will return to dust when we die. In Genesis 3:19 God says:

> *"In the sweat of your face you shall eat bread till you return to the ground, for out of it you were taken; for dust you are, and to dust you shall return."*

That fact alone should humble us.

Your body is a tent holding your spirit—which is the true you. Even though your body returns to dust when you die, your spirit immediately goes to be with the Lord, if you are a Christian. Ecclesiastes 12:7 says: *Then the dust will return to the earth as it was, and the spirit will return to God who gave it.*

After Death Comes Judgment

The next time you get upset, because you think someone is getting away with evil, remember, at the end of their life, they will be judged. When a non-believer dies, they not only go to hell, but they will also stand before God to be judged for every sin. Imagine every thought and deed done in the dark will be exposed in front of God. The Bible says every sin of a non-believer will be written down by God and judged:

And I saw the dead, small and great, standing before God, and books were opened. And another book was opened, which is the Book of Life. And the dead were judged according to their works, by the things which were written in the books. The sea gave up the dead who were in it, and Death and Hades delivered up the dead who were in them. And they were judged, each one according to his works (Revelation 20:12-13).

The Christian will have a far different experience at the judgment seat of Christ. We will NOT be judged for our sins, because Jesus Christ already paid the penalty for our sins on the Cross, so there is no need for us to be judged by God for our sins. That is good news. As a matter of fact, the psalmist declares: *As far as the east is from the west, so far has He removed our transgressions from us* (Psalm 103:12). God buries them in the deepest part of the ocean and remembers them no more (Psalm 103:16). This is why the Apostle Paul said:

There is therefore now no condemnation to those who are in Christ Jesus, who do not walk according to the flesh, but according to the Spirit (Romans 8:1).

Even though believers are not going to be judged for their sins, they will have a day of judgment. You and I will be judged for our motives. After we came to Christ, what was our motive in going to church; reading the Bible; studying God's Word; giving our money to God; witnessing; the way we treated people; and the way we loved people? Second Corinthians 5:10 says:

> *For we must all appear before the judgment seat of Christ,*
> *that each one may receive the things done in the body,*
> *according to what he has done, whether good or bad.*

This judgment will determine our rewards in heaven but will not affect our destination. We will go to heaven, because Christ paid for our sins on the Cross.

Eternal Life for Everyone

Everyone will die, and everyone will enter eternity. It is not just for Christians. We do not choose whether we will enter eternity or not, we only decide where we will spend eternity: heaven or hell and eventually the Lake of Fire. Job 14:14 says: *If a man dies, shall he live again? All the days of my hard service I will wait, till my change comes.*

Since we all get to choose whether we will spend eternity in heaven or in hell, it is important to understand what the Scriptures have to say about each place.

Heaven

Those who believe in Jesus Christ, and accepted Him as their Savior, will go to a literal place called heaven. John 3:5–7 says:

Jesus answered, "Most assuredly, I say to you, unless one is born of water and the Spirit, he cannot enter the kingdom of God. That which is born of the flesh is flesh, and that which is born of the Spirit is spirit. Do not marvel that I said to you, 'You must be born again.'"

Heaven is more than a city—a beautiful place; and it shines forth as exquisite jewels (Revelation 21:14-21). Jesus Christ resides with believers in heaven—being the very light illuminating heaven (Revelation 21:23). Those who have obeyed the Lord will enter the gates of the heavenly city. Revelation 22:14 says:

Blessed are those who do His commandments, that they may have the right to the tree of life, and may enter through the gates into the city.

When we get to heaven, all suffering will end. We will not remember the people we loved who did not go to heaven, because there is no sorrow in heaven. Revelation 21:4 says:

"And God will wipe away every tear from their eyes; there shall be no more death, nor sorrow, nor crying. There shall be no more pain, for the former things have passed away."

Then, after the Great White Throne Judgment, heaven and earth will pass away and God will create a new heaven and earth. Revelation 21:1 says:

> *Now I saw a new heaven and a new earth, for the first heaven and the first earth had passed away. Also there was no more sea.*

Everyone whose name was found in the Book of Life will enter into the new Heaven:

> *And He said to me, "It is done! I am the Alpha and the Omega, the Beginning and the End. I will give of the fountain of the water of life freely to him who thirsts. He who overcomes shall inherit all things, and I will be his God and he shall be My son* (Revelation 21:6-7).

This is a picture of eternity for the believer. Those who walk with Jesus Christ will inherit the new heaven and new earth.

Hell & the Lake of Fire

According to the Bible, if you were to die without Jesus Christ, you would go to a literal hell—a temporary holding place in the depths of the earth for the wicked. It is a place of torment, where men and women are separated from God.

In the Old Testament, the Hebrew word for *hell* is *Sheol* and is defined as "underworld, grave, hell or pit". The psalmist spoke of hell in Psalm 9:17: *The wicked shall be turned into hell, and all the nations that forget God,* and Psalm 55:15: *Let death seize them; let them go down alive into hell, for wickedness is in their dwellings and among them.*

In the New Testament, the word for *hell* is *Hades* in the Greek and it means, "the grave, death or hell." Jesus spoke about hell in Matthew 11:23: *"And you, Capernaum, who are exalted to heaven, will be brought down to Hades; for if the mighty works which were done in you had been done in Sodom, it would have remained until this day."*

While hell is beyond the worst thing your mind could imagine, it is not the end for those who reject Christ as their Savior. When John wrote the Book of Revelation, he revealed the final destination for the sinner is the Lake of Fire—a place of everlasting fire and torment— where they will be separated from Jesus forever and tormented eternally.

The Greek word for the *Lake of Fire* is *Gehenna*, used in the New Testament. Originally, the Lake of Fire was not made for humans. It was made for the devil and his demons, but men and women will reside there because they made the choice not to accept God's free gift of salvation. In Matthew 25:41, Jesus said:

"Then He will also say to those on the left hand, 'Depart from Me, you cursed, into the everlasting fire prepared for the devil and his angels:'"

The Lake of Fire is not a pleasant place. It is not a place where people go to party; it is a place where sinners will experience eternal punishment. John wrote about this judgment in Revelation 20:10:

> *The devil, who deceived them, was cast into the lake of fire and brimstone where the beast and the false prophet are. And they will be tormented day and night forever and ever.*

And again in Revelation 21:13-15:

> *The sea gave up the dead who were in it, and Death and Hades delivered up the dead who were in them. And they were judged, each one according to his works. Then Death and Hades were cast into the lake of fire. This is the second death. And anyone not found written in the Book of Life was cast into the lake of fire.*

While the Christian will spend eternity with Jesus in the new heaven and earth, those who ignored the free gift of salvation from the Lord will be cast into the Lake of Fire with Satan and his demons. The most important thing to remember is that the choice is ours—heaven or the Lake of Fire.

Understanding Death Helps You to Live

A person's beliefs on death determine how they live today. As Christians, we understand everything we own will burn one day.

You cannot take your checking account with you. You have never seen a hearse going to the cemetery with a U-Haul behind it.

The only thing you will be asked when you face God at the judgment seat is, "What did you do with My Son Jesus Christ?" That is why the Jesus says: *But seek first the kingdom of God and His righteousness, and all these things shall be added to you* (Matthew 6:33).

The person God uses has the right priorities and seeks to serve the Lord. They understand death and eternity—they have chosen heaven over hell. Jesus said:

> *He who loves his life will lose it, and he who hates his life in this world will keep it for eternal life. If anyone serves Me, let him follow Me; and where I am, there My servant will be also. If anyone serves Me, him My Father will honor* (John 12:25-26).

Chapter 11

The Person God Uses
Leads a Holy Life

I beseech you therefore, brethren, by the mercies of God,
that you present your bodies a living sacrifice, holy,
acceptable to God, which is your reasonable service.
Romans 12:1

The word *holy* is rarely used today—even in church. In an age where *morality* is a bad word—the very concept of holiness is foreign to most people. What does it truly mean to be holy?

In the Book of Romans, Paul told the Christians to present themselves as a living sacrifice, holy and acceptable to the Lord. Holy does not mean perfect; it means denying your fleshly desires and living a pure life before God.

In practical terms it means living according to God's Word, instead of bowing to peer pressure and giving in to temptation. Christians should care more about pleasing God and eternal life than satisfying their sinful fleshly desires. The Apostle Paul said to the Corinthians:

> *Therefore, having these promises, beloved, let us cleanse ourselves from all filthiness of the flesh and spirit, perfecting holiness in the fear of God* (2 Corinthians 7:1).

The word *holy* literally means "to be set apart." You and I have a calling from God to be set apart from others. We are not to follow the gods of this age and the values of this world, but rather, we are set apart to follow the Lord and His righteousness.

God has a purpose for your life, and He wants you to be in complete submission to Him—pursuing after His holiness on a daily basis. In pursuing holiness, we are called to be men and women of integrity, who are humble, obedient, sober and good stewards of all God has given us.

Joseph—Pursued Holiness

A man who pursued holiness and sought to please the Lord with his life was Joseph. He was a man God used greatly to deliver the children of Israel from the famine, but before he provided for Israel, he went through great trials. In his trials, he trusted in the Lord and lived a godly life.

Joseph did not have an easy life. He was sold by his brothers to the Egyptians as a slave. He ended up working for Potiphar, a eunuch in charge of the King's harem. Potiphar was impressed with Joseph's godly character. Even though Joseph was a servant in his home, Potiphar entrusted Joseph with a great deal of responsibility and treated him well.

Genesis 39:2 says: *The Lord was with Joseph, and he was a successful man; and he was in the house of his master the Egyptian.*

The presence of God was in Joseph's life—even in the midst of trials and difficulties. Joseph had a firm foundation in God—so he lived in holiness, set apart to the Lord.

Potiphar's wife was not a woman of integrity. She was attracted to Joseph, and made no attempt to hide it. Satan knew Joseph was close to God and the Lord was prospering him, so he tried to bring Joseph down and destroy him.

Often, when God is using your life and you are enjoying close fellowship with Him, Satan attacks the most. He does not want you to pursue holiness, so he tries to get you sidetracked with trials.

Satan saw an opportunity to tempt Joseph with Potiphar's wife. He hoped Joseph would sin and be separated from God, but Joseph was committed to God completely. He was also committed to serving Potiphar with integrity. Genesis 39:4 says: *So Joseph found favor in his sight, and served him. Then he made him overseer of his house, and all that he had he put under his authority.*

Potiphar was touched by the life of Joseph—he saw the hand of God upon him. Potiphar was not a believer, but he was greatly influenced by Joseph's godly lifestyle and character. God was using His holy servant as a witness to the nonbelievers.

While Potiphar had respect for Joseph and his life of integrity, his wife did not. She was after one thing—Joseph. Genesis 39:7 says: *And it came to pass after these things that his master's wife cast longing eyes on Joseph, and she said, "Lie with me."*

This was an immoral woman. She brazenly went after Joseph just like the immoral women in Proverbs 5:3-11:

> *For the lips of an immoral woman drip honey, and her mouth is smoother than oil; but in the end she is bitter as wormwood, sharp as a two-edged sword. Her feet go down to death, her steps lay hold of hell. Lest you ponder her path of life—her ways are unstable; you do not know them. Therefore hear me now, my children, and do not depart from the words of my mouth. Remove your way far from her, and do not go near the door of her house, lest you give your honor to others, and your years to the cruel one; lest aliens be filled with your wealth, and your labors go to the house of a foreigner; and you mourn at last, when your flesh and your body are consumed.*

Joseph knew God's law. He knew it was a sin to commit adultery. He honored and respected faithfulness in marriage, even though

Potiphar's wife did not. He responded to her, *"How then can I do this great wickedness, and sin against God?"* (Genesis 39:9).

Joseph could not betray God or Potiphar. He knew if he sinned, it would be against both God and man. Joseph understood he was being tempted; he understood the consequences, if he gave in to temptation; and he knew the sin would ultimately be against God.

Satan did not give up on Joseph. The woman kept coming after him, and Joseph kept ignoring her. Finally, she got desperate and bolder. Genesis 39:11-12 says:

> *But it happened about this time, when Joseph went into the house to do his work, and none of the men of the house was inside, that she caught him by his garment, saying, "Lie with me."*

This woman was very aggressive. She literally jumped on him and pulled at his clothes, but Joseph pulled away from her, losing his clothing, and ran out of the house.

Notice, Joseph did not stay in her room and try to reason with her. He ran away. He physically fled the temptation. Genesis 39:13-14 says:

> *And so it was, when she saw that he had left his garment in her hand and fled outside, that she called to the men of her house and spoke to them, saying, "See, he has brought in to us*

> *a Hebrew to mock us. He came in to me to lie with me, and*
> *I cried out with a loud voice.*

Joseph resisted the temptation, but was still blamed for attacking her. It does not seem fair; yet, Joseph did not worry about it. He knew God would defend him, and he was blameless before God. His concern was his standing before God, not before man.

Joseph's life was difficult. He did what was right and often received earthly punishment, but his life was in God's hands, and the Lord had a plan for him. Remember, Joseph ended up ruling over Egypt and was the person who saved his family and Israel from starvation. God used the difficulties in Joseph's life to make him the man he was—godly and successful.

Dr. Billy Graham said, "There is nothing unusual or abnormal about a Christian being tempted." Temptation is a part of life. It makes you strong; it builds integrity and character.

Doers of the Word

Joseph walked with the Lord, and it was evident in his life. He did not say he loved the Lord, and then live like a worldly person. He was a doer of the Word, as James exhorted the church: *But be doers of the word, and not hearers only, deceiving yourselves* (James 1:22).

Paul also exhorted the church in his letters, especially to the Corinthians. They had accepted Jesus Christ as their Savior, but were living carnal lives. They were not fully committed to the holiness of God, as they allowed a man living in sexual sin with his fathers wife to remain in the church. Since Paul was not in Corinth, he wrote a letter to the Christian leaders questioning their integrity and commitment to the teaching of Jesus Christ.

What was happening in the Corinthian church is happening in many churches today, because pastors are afraid to speak against sin. They are afraid to offend people and lose members.

Paul saw the danger in ignoring the sin. Allowing the church member to flagrantly live in a very immoral situation, while claiming to be Christian, was poisoning the other Christians in the church. It also served as a bad witness to the nonbelievers in the community.

People are watching us. They watch what we say, what we do and how we react. When you say you are a believer you will be watched, because people want to see if your faith is real.

You are God's representative to a world in darkness. You need to be holy and have integrity in your life. You need to be accountable to others. Many Christians do not want to be responsible for their actions. If you watch the news, you will see the lack of integrity in this world. It is rare to see a leader who has moral integrity. In these evil days, it is even more important for Christians to be an example. The darker this world gets, the brighter our lights should shine.

As a Christian, you are not only representing Christ to the world, if you are a parent, you have little disciples watching you all the time.

It is important for you to take the Word of God literally and make adjustments in your life to reflect the holiness and righteousness of God.

As Christians, we are to be an example of the holiness of Christ—we are to be a light in a dark world. Francis of Assisi said, "Preach the gospel at all times. If necessary, use words."

Imitate God

If you want to live your life in holiness, you need to imitate God. God is holy, and we are to imitate Him. Peter said: *but as He who called you is holy, you also be holy in all your conduct, because it is written, "Be holy, for I am holy"* (1 Peter 1:15-16).

It is not easy to imitate God, but through His Word, He has given us all we need to be Christ-like. In imitating Christ, we will be holy men and women, pursuing the things of God, not the things of our flesh or the world.

If you stick with the Lord, and you are faithful and obedient to His Word, you are going to glorify the Lord. Look at what Peter said to the church in his first letter.

> *But you are a chosen generation, a royal priesthood, a holy nation, His own special people, that you may proclaim the praises of Him who called you out of darkness into His marvelous light; who once were not a people but are now the people of God, who had not obtained mercy but now*

have obtained mercy. Beloved, I beg you as sojourners and pilgrims, abstain from fleshly lusts which war against the soul, having your conduct honorable among the Gentiles, that when they speak against you as evildoers, they may, by your good works which they observe, glorify God in the day of visitation (1 Peter 2:9-12).

Living Holy in Humility

If you are pursuing holiness in your life, you have great integrity before believers and non-believers, and as Joseph, you will be men and women of humility.

Webster's dictionary defines the word *humble* as "not to be proud or not to be arrogant." A humble person is more interested in others, not looking for recognition or to be promoted. In fact, a truly humble person depends on God.

In the New Testament, the word for *humble* means "being subservient—low in rank, status, or position." We often think a humble person is shy, speaks softly, looks down at the ground and is kind of wimpy, but that is not a true picture of humility. A humble person is someone who esteems others above himself and has an attitude of service.

When you look at the Bible, Jesus Christ stands out as a true example of humility. In every encounter He had with people, He put their needs before His own. A great example of how Jesus put the needs of the people before His own is the feeding of the five thousand in Matthew 14:13-16:

> *When Jesus heard it, He departed from there by boat to a deserted place by Himself. But when the multitudes heard it, they followed Him on foot from the cities. And when Jesus went out He saw a great multitude; and He was moved with compassion for them, and healed their sick. When it was evening, His disciples came to Him, saying, "This is a deserted place, and the hour is already late. Send the multitudes away, that they may go into the villages and buy themselves food." But Jesus said to them, "They do not need to go away. You give them something to eat."*

Jesus had just heard of the death of John the Baptist and He departed from the people to spend some time alone. He was greatly saddened but the death of John. While He needed time alone, the multitude followed Him and He was moved with compassion for them. Even though He was mourning, He put His feelings aside and ministered to the multitude.

In His great humility, Christ never put Himself above others. He was the Son of God, He denied His own needs and wants, in order to serve the needs of others.

Pride of Life

Many times, people think they are humble. They tell everyone they know how humble they are—which tells me they are prideful, because they like people to think they serve others. If we truly want to be humble servants of the Lord, we have to recognize pride in ourselves and in others. Proverbs 16:18-19 says:

Pride goes before destruction, and a haughty spirit before a fall. Better to be of a humble spirit with the lowly, than to divide the spoil with the proud.

The greatest example of a prideful life and the complete opposite of Christ's humility is found in the pride of Lucifer. Pride is destructive and it destroyed Lucifer.

Lucifer was the most beautiful being in heaven. God created him to be the worship leader, but Lucifer got caught up in his position. Pride filled his heart and before long he declared himself to be greater than God—that is pride!

In Isaiah 14:13-15, God confronted Lucifer's lofty claims:

"For you have said in your heart: 'I will ascend into heaven, I will exalt my throne above the stars of God; I will also sit on the mount of the congregation on the farthest sides of the north; I will ascend above the heights of the clouds, I will be like the Most High.' Yet you shall be brought down to Sheol, to the lowest depths of the Pit."

God did not allow Lucifer to make these claims, without consequences. Because he would not humble himself before the

Lord, God made it clear his final outcome would be the Lake of Fire.

That is why Satan hates God—and hates His people. The sin of pride destroyed Satan and he uses pride to destroy countless people, by enticing them with the things of this world. John said: *For all that is in the world—the lust of the flesh, the lust of the eyes, and the pride of life—is not of the Father but is of the world* (1 John 2:16).

Choose to Be Used

Throughout Scriptures, there are examples of people who have been ruined by pride. Both Pharaoh and Nebachudnezzar were filled with pride and refused to humble themselves before God. Over and over again, the Bible gives examples of how pride destroys people.

In contrast, the Bible also gives us many examples of people who have been greatly used by God, as humble servants. Joseph, David, Paul the Apostle, Peter and many others humbled themselves before the Lord and God used their lives to build the Kingdom of God.

C.S. Lewis said: "There are only two classes of people: those who say to God, 'Thy will be done,' and those to whom God finally says, 'Thy will be done.'"

Eventually, we all choose—humility or pride—but if we choose to be prideful, God will humble us.

The Importance of Stewardship

As servants of the Lord, God has called us to give to the work of the Lord. Everything we have belongs to Him: our jobs, time, money and our abilities—we did not create these things on our own. The money we spend, the time we spend and the gifts and talents we use are all given to us by God, to give glory and honor to the Lord. Proverbs 3:9-10 says:

> *Honor the Lord with your possessions, and with the firstfruits of all your increase; so your barns will be filled with plenty, and your vats will overflow with new wine.*

We do not give to God because He is in need. God is not broke, because He owns everything. He owns you and He owns me; He owns everything on this earth. The psalmist wrote: *For every beast of the forest is Mine, and the cattle on a thousand hills* (Psalm 50:10). God does not need anything from me, but all I have belongs to Him.

Give in Worship to God

In the Book of Deuteronomy, Moses told the children of Israel to give to the Lord in worship:

> *"Then you shall set it before the Lord your God, and worship before the Lord your God. So you shall rejoice in every good thing which the Lord your God has given to you and your house, you and the Levite and the stranger who is among you* (Deuteronomy 26:10-11).

They were to rejoice in all the good things the Lord had given to them and done for them. Notice the word *rejoice*. They did not give to the Lord grudgingly but joyfully, knowing it all belonged to the Lord and He graciously provided for all their needs.

When we give in worship of the Lord, our hearts are right with Him. King David understood the need to give to God with a willing and sacrificial heart:

> *Then King David said to Ornan, "No, but I will surely buy it for the full price, for I will not take what is yours for the Lord, nor offer burnt offerings with that which costs me nothing"* (1 Chronicles 21:24).

In the New Testament, Paul told the church to give to the Lord with willing hearts, because He looks at our motives and our heart more than the gift itself. *So let each one give as he purposes in his heart, not grudgingly or of necessity; for God loves a cheerful giver* (2 Corinthians 9:7).

Generous Servants
As we serve the Lord, He will provide for all of our needs, but we decide how we will manage what He provides. As good house stewards, we have a responsibility to manage all he has given to us wisely. God holds us responsible. He keeps a record of all we do in heaven. The things we do for the Lord in this life carry the weight of glory in heaven!

Pastor Chuck Smith always said, "Only what you do for Christ will last, period!"

Holy and Sober

When God calls a Christian to serve Him, He calls them to holiness. If Christians are to live holy and set apart from the Lord, they cannot cling to the things of this world. Jesus explained this to the disciples in Luke 21:34:

> "But take heed to yourselves, lest your hearts be weighed down with carousing, drunkenness, and cares of this life, and that Day come on you unexpectedly. You will not be ready when the Lord comes because you are not sober. You will be passed out or be drinking. You will be judged by God. No drunkard will ever inherit the kingdom of God."

This is a controversial topic because many churches teach and believe you can drink alcohol, but Jesus, Himself, said you cannot serve the Lord unless you are sober.

Jesus was not the first to teach against drinking. It goes back to the Old Testament. Solomon wrote:

> It is not for kings, O Lemuel, it is not for kings to drink wine, nor for princes intoxicating drink; lest they drink and forget the law, and pervert the justice of all the afflicted (Proverbs 31:4-5).

Isaiah taught:

> *Woe to those who rise early in the morning, that they may follow intoxicating drink; who continue until night, till wine inflames them!* (Isaiah 5:11).

Hosea said: *"Harlotry, wine, and new wine enslave the heart"* (Hosea 4:11).

Churches and pastors can teach in favor of drinking, but the Word of God overwhelmingly contradicts their belief. In the Bible, wine and strong drinks are often connected with immorality. They can control your heart and mind.

God called us to deny ourselves and our fleshly desires. He is not looking for immoral servants. He is looking for holy servants. To be a servant, used by God, we cannot serve God and the flesh. It is impossible. We must be willing to submit our lives to Him—fully and completely.

Obedience

It seems like there is so much you need to know to be a person God uses, but in reality, it comes down to obedience. When you are obedient to the Lord and the things He has given to us in His Word, you will seek to know Him, to serve Him and to abide in Him.

A person can study the Bible and memorize Scriptures, but if the Word does not live in them, they only have head knowledge and God cannot use them. He is looking for men and women who have real heart knowledge of Him. Jesus said:

> *Abide in Me, and I in you. As the branch cannot bear fruit of itself, unless it abides in the vine, neither can you, unless you abide in Me. "I am the vine, you are the branches. He who abides in Me, and I in him, bears much fruit; for without Me you can do nothing* (John 15:4-5).

When we come to the end of ourselves, and realize the only way we can truly serve Him is by denying our flesh, He will abide in us and use our lives in ways we cannot ever imagine.

It is God's desire that we would be blameless and holy. Ephesians 1:4 says: *just as He chose us in Him before the foundation of the world, that we should be holy and without blame before Him in love.*

God loves you. We should humble ourselves in His presence and lift up holy hands and give the Lord our whole life.

Chapter 12

The Person God Uses
The Perfect Servant: Jesus

When He had been baptized, Jesus came up immediately from the water; and behold, the heavens were opened to Him, and He saw the Spirit of God descending like a dove and alighting upon Him. And suddenly a voice came from heaven, saying, "This is My beloved Son, in whom I am well pleased."
Matthew 3:16-17

Throughout this book, we have looked at examples of people God used—His servants. From the Old Testament to the New Testament, God used flawed human beings to serve Him and further the Kingdom of God. None of them were perfect and none of them could claim to know or be obedient in all the areas addressed in the book. They were merely willing, obedient servants of the Lord—no different than you and me.

I am so thankful for those flawed servants, because they encourage me. Their lives are reminders of who is truly doing the work—

149

God! They also encourage me to get back up when I mess up, because God still wants to use me.

However, there is one perfect Servant the Lord used and continues to use today—Jesus Christ. There has never been another servant like Him and no one will ever fully compare to Him.

As Christians, we are called to be like Him. He is our standard and example. While we can never be perfect and complete here on earth, we have His life as an example of how God would like us to live our lives. Paul the Apostle really understood Jesus was his example. He said: *Imitate me, just as I also imitate Christ* (1 Corinthian 11:1).

If we go through the chapters of this book, only Christ fulfills every qualification. He not only understands salvation, but He is salvation:

> *Therefore I endure all things for the sake of the elect, that they also may obtain the salvation which is in Christ Jesus with eternal glory* (2 Timothy 2:10).

And our Redeemer:

> *But of Him you are in Christ Jesus, who became for us wisdom from God—and righteousness and sanctification and redemption—*(1 Corinthians 1:30).

Grace and mercy flows through Him:

Grace, mercy, and peace will be with you from God the Father and from the Lord Jesus Christ, the Son of the Father, in truth and love (2 John 1:3).

By faith, He submitted to the Father's will and went to the Cross for us: counting the cost as no other has done:

And He said, "Abba, Father, all things are possible for You. Take this cup away from Me; nevertheless, not what I will, but what You will" (Mark 14:36).

He has been with the Holy Spirit from the beginning and knows Him and the Father intimately: *In the beginning God* [Elohim] *created the heavens and the earth* (Genesis 1:1).

He was a man of prayer:

Jesus spoke these words, lifted up His eyes to heaven, and said: "Father, the hour has come. Glorify Your Son, that Your Son also may glorify You (John 17:1).

He knew the Word, because He is the Word: *In the beginning was the Word, and the Word was with God, and the Word was God* (John 1:1).

Jesus came to this world to save us because He loves us so much:

By this we know love, because He laid down His life for us. ... (1 John 3:16), and forgives us of our sins: *Him God has exalted to His right hand to be Prince and Savior, to give repentance to Israel and forgiveness of sins* (Acts 5:31).

Even the demons recognized the holiness of Jesus: saying, *"Let us alone! What have we to do with You, Jesus of Nazareth? Did You come to destroy us? I know who You are—the Holy One of God!"* (Mark 1:24)

God has called you to be His servant. He has called you to be Christ-like—a Christian, a follower of His Son. He has not called you to be Jesus. It is not possible. Only Jesus could fulfill the Word of God. Only He could be redemption for a world of lost souls.

If you are a servant, a person used by God, all you have to do is point people to Jesus, the perfect Servant. Who rescues the sinner and provides the way to eternal life.

Are you ready to be used by God? Do you want to be a disciple of Jesus Christ? Then, follow Him...

Then He said to them, "Follow Me, and I will make you fishers of men" (Matthew 4:19).

Somebody Loves You Media Group

BOOKS:

Raul Ries
From Fury to Freedom (Revised)
MAN: Natural, Carnal, Spiritual
IMPURITY: The Naked Truth
SIN: The Root of All Evil
OBEDIENCE: Waking Up to God Devotional
DOCTRINES: A Simplified Road Map of Biblical Truth
Seven Steps to a Successful Marriage
Raising a Godly Family in an Ungodly World
Somebody Loves You Growth Book
30 Questions that Deserve Answers
Practical Living from God's Word Devotional
Follow Me (Kindle Only)
Understanding God's Compassion
Five Deadly Vices (Kindle Only)
Living Above Your Circumstances:
          A Study in the Book of Daniel
God Answers Prayer (Kindle Only)
Hear What the Spirit Is Saying

Sharon Ries
The Well-Trodden Path
My Husband, My Maker

Other Authors:
Patriarcas en la Carcel by Ruth Smith
The Philosophy of Ministry of Calvary Chapel by Chuck Smith
The Night Cometh by Edmund and Naomi Farrel

FILMS IN DVD*

Raul Ries:
Fury to Freedom
Taking the Hill: Special 2-DVD Package
Taking the Hill
A Quiet Hope
A Venture in Faith:
    The History and Philosophy of the Calvary Chapel
    Movement

*All DVD's are in English and Spanish

Somebody Loves You Media Group
22324 Golden Springs Drive
Diamond Bar, CA 91765-2449

(909) 859-6508
slymg@calvarygs.org
www.calvarygs.org